"No platitudes here. Down-to-earth, realistic, and above all else, freeing. Scott Morton shares practical insights that will help you take sensible steps to connect with the heart of the Lord."

—REV. ELLIS F. GOLDSTEIN,
masters of biblical studies, director of ministry partner development,
Campus Crusade for Christ

"In the midst of so many self-help books, Scott's new book stands out as a strong dose of 'God sense' that leads us toward that freedom we all long for."

— BETTY BARNETT,
YWAM missionary; author of *Friend Raising*;
YWAM managing editor for Zondervan's *Christian Growth Study Bible*

"Scott has reimagined for us what simply following Jesus can look like in every area of life—that is, once we stop trying and begin trusting."

MICHAEL CARD, musician; teacher;
author of *A Sacred Sorrow*

"Thank you, Scott, for modeling such a healthy life perspective and challenging us to join you in facing and growing out of our hindering misconceptions."

—BILL THRALL, cofounder, Leadership Catalyst;
coauthor of *The Ascent of a Leader* and *TrueFaced*

"With a transparent and conversational tone backed up by years of investing in people, Scott Morton breathes new life into the journey of spiritual transformation in Christ."

—MARK L. EARLEY,
president and CEO, Prison Fellowship

tired of
do-list
christianity?

Debunking the
Misconceptions that
Hold Back Spiritual Growth
and Steal Your Joy!

SCOTT MORTON

NAVPRESS®

BRINGING TRUTH TO LIFE

The Navigators is an international Christian organization. Our mission is to advance the gospel of Jesus and His kingdom into the nations through spiritual generations of laborers living and discipling among the lost. We see a vital movement of the gospel, fueled by prevailing prayer, flowing freely through relational networks and out into the nations where workers for the kingdom are next door to everywhere.

NavPress is the publishing ministry of The Navigators. The mission of NavPress is to reach, disciple, and equip people to know Christ and make Him known by publishing life-related materials that are biblically rooted and culturally relevant. Our vision is to stimulate spiritual transformation through every product we publish.

© 2006 by Scott Morton

All rights reserved. No part of this publication may be reproduced in any form without written permission from NavPress, P.O. Box 35001, Colorado Springs, CO 80935.
www.navpress.com

NAVPRESS, BRINGING TRUTH TO LIFE, and the NAVPRESS logo are registered trademarks of NavPress. Absence of ® in connection with marks of NavPress or other parties does not indicate an absence of registration of those marks.

ISBN 1-57683-796-3

Cover design by Arvid Wallen
Cover photo by Graham French/Masterfile
Creative Team: Don Simpson, Keith Wall, Darla Hightower, Judy Wilson, Pat Reinheimer, Kathy Guist

Some of the anecdotal illustrations in this book are true to life and are included with the permission of the persons involved. All other illustrations are composites of real situations, and any resemblance to people living or dead is coincidental.

Unless otherwise identified, all Scripture quotations in this publication are taken from the the the *New American Standard Bible* (NASB), © The Lockman Foundation 1960, 1962, 1963, 1968, 1971, 1972, 1973, 1975, 1977, 1995. Other versions include: the HOLY BIBLE: NEW INTERNATIONAL VERSION® (NIV®). Copyright © 1973, 1978, 1984 by International Bible Society, used by permission of Zondervan Publishing House, all rights reserved.

Library of Congress Cataloging-in-Publication Data
Morton, Scott.
 Tired of do-list Christianity? : debunking the misconceptions that
hold back spiritual growth and steal your joy / Scott Morton.
     p. cm.
 Includes bibliographical references.
 ISBN 1-57683-796-3
 1. Christian life. 2. Spiritual life--Christianity. 3. Spiritual formation. I. Title.
 BV4501.3.M6743 2006
 248.4--dc22
                        2006007026

Printed in the United States of America

1 2 3 4 5 6 / 10 09 08 07 06

FOR A FREE CATALOG OF NAVPRESS BOOKS & BIBLE STUDIES,
CALL 1-800-366-7788 (USA) OR 1-800-839-4769 (CANADA)

Contents

Introduction: Airport Road Doesn't Lead to the Airport   7

PART ONE: Misconceptions About Spiritual Disciplines

1. Having a Belief System Is Enough   13
2. Daily Quiet Time—Daily Blessing   17
3. To Be Transformed, Focus on Behavior Modification   21
4. Spiritual Disciplines: Work, Work, Work   26
5. Growing in Prayer: I've Already Tried   31

PART TWO: Misconceptions About Temptation

6. Once You've Dealt with a Particular Sin, It's Gone Forever   37
7. Growing Christians Focus on Sinning Less   41
8. Confessing the Visible Sin Resolves It   45
9. Ogling Women Is a "Guy Thing"—It Can't Be Helped   49
10. You'll Always Be a People-Pleaser   53

PART THREE: Misconceptions About Personal Ministry

11. Only Your Spiritual Service Makes a Difference in the World   59
12. To Spread the Gospel, You Must Be Eloquent   63
13. Sharing Your Faith Will Always Be an Awkward "Have-to"   67
14. Avoid Worldliness—Stay in the Holy Huddle   71

PART FOUR: Misconceptions About Emotional Health

15. Committed Christians Don't Get Discouraged   77
16. Fear Is Only for Wimpy Christians   81
17. Everyone Worries Sometimes—What's the Big Deal?   85
18. Harboring a Little Resentment Can't Hurt   90
19. Your Self-Esteem Is Determined by Others   94

PART FIVE: Misconceptions About Your Schedule

20. Sure, You're Busy — It's Unavoidable   101
21. You Need to Be Available 24/7   105

PART SIX: Misconceptions About Relationships

22. You Can't Help But Be a Little Judgmental   111
23. If It Blesses You, It Will Bless Others   115
24. Leadership Is Primarily Talking   119
25. Always Have An Agenda   122

PART SEVEN: Misconceptions About Family Expectations

26. Good Parents Never Resent Their Children   127
27. Falling Out of Love? It's Over   131
28. Great Parenting Guarantees Great Kids   136

PART EIGHT: Misconceptions About Your Body

29. You Are What You Look Like   143
30. Denial Is the Best Way to Handle Aging   146
31. No Heaven-Bound Person Should Be Afraid of Dying   150

PART NINE: Misconceptions About Generally Accepted Rules

32. Tithing Is the Standard   155
33. Skipping Church Is No Big Deal   159
34. God Expects 110 Percent   163
35. God's Will Is Tough to Figure Out   167

PART TEN: Misconceptions About Integrity Issues

36. Your Outer Life Dictates Your Character   173
37. Financial Decisions Are Not Spiritual Decisions   177
38. If It Seems Right, It Can't Be Wrong   180

Conclusion: Spiritual Growth Starts with Your Thinking   184

Notes   186

About the Author   189

airport road doesn't lead to the airport

T HE BOOK YOU HOLD IN YOUR hands reveals thirty-eight big and little misconceptions that stifle our joy, undermine our relationships, and make us wonder if we truly can be transformed into Christ's image. Identifying misconceptions sounds simple enough, but be careful. We have grown comfortable with old patterns of thinking—like well-worn dusty cow paths in the pastures of our minds. Why is genuine spiritual transformation so elusive?

Something is wrong with spiritual growth among believers today. We want to become more like Christ, but it's not happening—at least not for many. As author Dallas Willard says, "Faith today is treated as something that only *should* make us different, not that actually does or can make us different. Our faith should make us different, but it's only a theory for most."[1] For many of us being transformed into the image of Christ is more fantasy than reality, wishful thinking rather than an actual occurrence.

To combat this malaise, believers are "pounded" (as a newly converted friend of mine puts it) to do better, to try harder, or be more committed. We hear it not only from sermons, but also from books, seminars, and well-meaning friends. We're weary of being pressured and strong-armed, so to protect ourselves we are developing Sunday morning immunity against "being more committed."

But is being more committed the answer to every problem? Millions of believers *are* deeply committed—or were—but they wonder if their lives can truly change year by year. They point to immediate changes the first year they took Christ seriously, but there's been little transformation since.

Being more committed has merit, but it is an oversimplified solution. Something else is stifling Christlike change—and it is not complicated. Misguided notions and crippling misconceptions about spiritual growth and the Christian life stifle progress. We all have faulty assumptions and erroneous thought patterns, but most are hidden from us. It is time to discover them and think differently.

Think of it this way: If I am new to town and see a street called Airport Road, I assume it will lead to the airport. But in the town where I live, that would be a bad assumption. Airport Road does *not,* in fact, go to the airport (but that's another story for another time).

Now let's suppose I don't know the truth about the inaccurately named Airport Road. In frustration, I call from my cell phone to say that I can't find the airport. You suggest I be more committed to locating it.

"Rededicate yourself to finding it, and try harder," you tell me. "Deepen your commitment to the cause!"

So I drive Airport Road more earnestly, looking intently for airport signs or other assistance that will get me to my destination. But your advice doesn't help because your beginning assumption was in error, too. You see the trap I am in. My "counselors" have the same misconceptions that I do and cannot help.

As I grow tired of trying harder, I'll conclude (as Dallas Willard suggests) that getting to the airport is "only a theory." Or, that getting to the airport is only for specially gifted travelers more committed than I.

Similarly, if our faith is to make us different, we must discover the misconceptions and faulty assumptions that hold us back—bad thinking! I believe this is what the apostle Paul was getting at when he said, "be transformed by the renewing of your *mind*" (Romans 12:2 emphasis added).

As you launch into discovering your own misconceptions, don't worry about whether you are "committed enough." In fact, let's assume you aren't. (There, that issue is resolved!) Instead, look honestly at what needs to work better in your walk with Christ and in your relationships with people. This time, instead of trying harder or "working on it," try *thinking* differently. Break out across the pasture and get on a different road—one that leads to your destination!

Are you tired of do-list Christianity—trying to complete lots of tasks, check off the right items on the list, and do all the right things? I'm guessing that you have a few (perhaps more) misconceptions about the Christian faith that hinder your growth and steal your joy. In the pages that follow, we're going to explore some fallacies and false assumptions that believers don't talk about much—issues that have plagued us our whole lives. Let's bring them into the open. Some misconceptions you'll recognize; others may surprise you. Acknowledging some will bring relief, while confronting others will be painful to admit. Thinking differently will seem odd for a time, but it will turn to exhilaration as you continue to tell yourself the truth.

You'll see quickly in the personal stories that follow that I don't have it "all figured out." In sharing my struggles, I hope you'll not only admit that you don't have it figured out either, but also that God will show you any crippling misconceptions that hold you back.

I welcome you as a fellow explorer.

misconceptions about spiritual disciplines

having a belief system is enough

OKAY, A CONFESSION: I START EACH day intending to walk deeply with God, but sometimes it's three o'clock in the afternoon before I remember I'm a Christian. In my busy office, I've had no thought of God, and it hasn't occurred to me to pray over the pile on my desk. The minutes spin by so quickly.

On those days, I call myself a "Creedal Christian"—one who attends church regularly, reads the Bible, and can reasonably articulate the Christian position on social issues. But am I following a system rather than experiencing a Savior? Am I adhering to creeds or am I encountering Christ?

I discovered the difference between a Creedal Christian and an "experiencing Christian" in the mountains around Breckenridge, Colorado, where I spend three days each year alone with the Lord. I wish I could tell you I withdraw from people and food for seventy-two hours. But holing up in a secluded mountain cabin in September, alone with my Bible, my unusable cell phone, and Hershey candy bars amidst bears bulking up for the winter doesn't work for me.

Actually, it happened like this: A few years ago in a nice Breckenridge B&B, I read a section in a workbook on prayer that instructed, "Jot down your answers to prayer in the past week."

I couldn't think of any. I reread the instructions. Nothing. I panicked. Surely, a devoted Christian can write down answers to prayer. I consulted my journal. I expanded the time frame, going back two weeks, then a month. Still nothing.

Frantically scanning my journal, I finally found a six-month-old answer to a prayer so trivial I was almost embarrassed I recorded it. But because it became a personal benchmark about experiencing God, I'll share it.

Early one March morning (six months before my Breckenridge retreat), I felt overwhelmed by the blizzard of work activities coming my way. So I prayed through each item in my daily planner one by one. I particularly prayed over a phone call I needed to make to a hard-nosed salesman, "Jeffrey," to remind him to send his quarterly $500 ministry gift. Even though he asked me to remind him, I felt like I was nagging. I procrastinated. I transferred the notation *Call Jeffrey* to the following Monday for six consecutive weeks. Then one day, I determined to push fear and busyness aside to phone Jeffrey.

At the office, I handled a couple of urgent requests and then opened my planner. *Call Jeffrey. Now!* As I leaned down to my briefcase for his number, the phone rang. It was Jeffrey!

"Hey, Scott, how are you doing?" he said.

"Great, Jeffrey. I was just thinking of you," I gushed in disbelief.

"Yeah, me, too. Hey, I just put a check in the mail for $1,000 to catch up on my giving. I wanted to make sure I had the right account number."

In shock, I told Jeffrey I was in the process of phoning him. We went on to have a good conversation. What a *coincidence*!

The next day, another shock came. I was late scheduling appointments for a trip to Michigan and needed to buy an airplane ticket immediately. But I couldn't until I confirmed an appointment with Rick, who had not responded to a note I sent him a month earlier.

Determined not to procrastinate, I reached for Rick's phone number just as the phone rang. It was Rick. He asked if he could accompany me to Grand Rapids. That's just what I was hoping for.

Back to my prayer workbook in Breckenridge. Now I was on a roll, quickly jotting down other "coincidences" as specifically as I could, surprised to see that my ignored coincidences happened frequently. I gave them an acronym:

HUAGs: Highly Unusual Acts of God

I came back from Breckenridge determined to experience God in little things — the way I had as a new believer.

But because I was leery about seeing "signs from God" behind every change in the weather, I checked with an older mentor, whose many years of walking with God had earned my respect. After telling him about my HUAGs over fried rice at a favorite Chinese eatery, I asked, "Is it coincidence or is it God?"

He fixed a piercing gaze directly on me and said confidently, "Scott, it's God!"

Today, I see God in little things. But don't misunderstand. I'm not looking for assurances that He is with me. He has promised that in the Scriptures. My problem is overlooking the quiet activity of God in daily life because I'm too hurried, too worried, too buried.

Paying attention to little things reminds me of Brother Lawrence (1611 — 1691), who served in the Carmelite Order in France. Born Nicholas Herman to peasant parents in Lorraine, he became a professional soldier during the Thirty Years' War in Europe, during which he suffered a severe leg wound that gave him a lifelong limp. He entered the service of the Carmelites in 1651 and cooked in the monastery kitchen for fifteen years. He is known for the phrase "practicing the presence of God."

Does practicing the presence of God mean thinking about God every waking minute? Brother Lawrence did not advocate that. Instead, he exhorts us to discipline our minds to return to God when we are not disposed with necessary matters—much as a lover longs for her espoused. He also said:

> That time of business does not with me differ from the time of prayer, and in the noise and clatter of my kitchen, while several persons are at the same time calling for different things, I possess God in as great tranquility as if I were upon my knees at the blessed sacrament.[1]

By contrast, understanding the creed and acting the way Christians are supposed to act is not the same as experiencing God. When we practice the presence of God, we consciously seek to be in tune with what He is doing—especially in HUAGs—like "coincidental" phone calls.

How about you? Are you stuck in the misconception that the Christian life is primarily believing the right things about God and staying busy—a system? Or are you experiencing the presence of God before three o'clock in the afternoon? What Highly Unusual Acts of God have come your way today?

daily quiet time — daily blessing

W HEN I WAS A NEW CHRISTIAN, I heard people say cheerfully, "When I have a quiet time first thing in the morning, my day goes great. And on those days when I skip my morning devotions, my day goes badly."

That sounded reasonable. So I determined to start a routine of quiet times every morning. After all, who wants a lousy day?

My devotions went fine for a week — seven for seven! And my days went well, too. A good quiet time ensures a good day. This really works! Or so I thought.

Then one morning, I woke up late with barely enough time to make an early appointment across town. Rather than arrive late, I guiltily prayed in the car as I hurried through traffic. Quiet time "lite." I expected my day to go poorly. I imagined that by 5:00 p.m. my car would spew icky black stuff and a new species of termites would be found in the walls of my house.

But my day went fine. No car problems, no ravaging insects. Hmm.

Many years have passed since those early days of learning to walk with Christ, and my "good devotions equals good day" theory has *not* proven true. I've experienced great early-morning quiet times but ended up having lousy days. And I've skipped early-morning devotions (sometimes on purpose) but enjoyed wonderful days of blessing. What is it that I don't know about God?

So what is a reasonable batting average for daily devotions? Six out of seven per week? Three out of seven? Three hundred and two out of three hundred and sixty-five days, with Saturdays and holidays off?

I once met a man from Michigan who said he had not missed a daily quiet time in more than twenty years—7,300 consecutive days! Though he exuded Christlike peace with his quiet demeanor, I suspiciously began looking for signs of legalism. Finally, I asked him if he did it out of obligation. He replied, "I just enjoy spending time with the Lord."

By contrast, I have met believers who are equally freed up who do not attempt to have devotions daily. Nor are they concerned about the time of day they have them—sometimes in the morning, sometimes at night, sometimes at midday.

Measuring Christian maturity by means of a devotional batting average misses the point, but in surveys of evangelicals conducted by The Navigators, "improving daily devotions" consistently shows up as a top goal. Why the struggle? I think it's time to discard four misconceptions.

First, the Bible does not *command* daily quiet times. Perhaps the most famous passage on a daily quiet time is Psalm 5:3:

In the morning, O LORD, Thou wilt hear my voice;
In the morning I will order my prayer to Thee and eagerly watch.

This wonderful passage is an example, not a command. Not surprisingly, we read that Jesus rose early in the morning to go out to a lonely place to pray (see Mark 1:35). If Jesus and David disciplined themselves to begin their days in prayer, shouldn't you and I? Probably, but it is not the 11th commandment. I get the idea that Jesus and David spent time with the Father because they wanted to — not out of duty. Suppose you told your daughter, "Meet me every morning at 6:00 a.m. for twenty minutes to prove how much you love me." Ludicrous. Devotions go way beyond duty.

Second, morning is not the only time for devotions. Many "non-morning people" feel defeated by the assumption that morning is the best time to commune with God. Because they struggle to meet the Lord at 6:00 a.m., they give up on meeting Him at all. But David and Jesus also sought the Lord's presence throughout the day and even in the night hours.

Third, having a quiet time does not guarantee a great day. Equating God's blessing with my daily contribution of half-hour devotions is a poorly disguised good-works mentality. For perspective, I wonder if David had morning devotions the day his son, Absalom, launched an insurrection against him. Tough day!

The fourth and most damaging misconception is the unspoken goal of trying to "get something" out of a quiet time. Is the purpose of a quiet time to get a "thought for the day" or direction for a problem or to find God's will? This leads to a common devotional practice:

"The Flying Fickle Finger of Faith"

It goes like this: Close your eyes, flop open the Bible, plop your finger on a random verse, open your eyes, and read the verse closest to your finger. That is God's direction for the day . . . or confirmation of a marriage partner . . . or affirmation to buy a new house. Though God can speak through this method, it reveals a preoccupation with trying to know *God's will* more than trying to know *God Himself*. It also positions God as a celestial advisor rather than the One worthy of worship.

My devotional life changed when I switched from trying to *get something* out of each quiet time to simply seeking the Lord in worship. I no longer must have a "word from God." Nor do I search for a key verse or direction for a thorny problem. These days I simply begin my devotions with expectation of enjoying God's presence. I've stopped asking, "What did I get out of my quiet time?" I now ask, "What did the Lord get out of my quiet time?" Did He hear me praising Him or surrendering my will?

What about the everyday thing? Unlike my Michigan friend, I don't meet with the Lord every day, nor are my quiet times always in the morning. But they do happen *almost* every morning, simply because I want to be with the One who gave Himself for me. Sometimes they last five minutes, but usually they are much longer. And sometimes, I drive out on the prairies on Sunday afternoons just to be with Him.

What about you? If you find it difficult to meet the Lord every day, ponder the four misconceptions I've described. Is one or more holding you back? Change your assumptions and try again. When we walk with God in a worshipful and reverent relationship, tracking our devotional batting average becomes unnecessary.

CHAPTER 3

to be transformed, focus on behavior modification

JUST READ A BOOK BY the pollster George Barna, who said, "Once children reach the age of twelve or so, the chances of changing how they think and believe are limited. The chance of changing adults is very slim."[1]

I find this discouraging. Is the transforming power of God available only to those eleven years old and younger? Can't adults change?

However, we see daily that Barna is right. Some Christians who have graduated from discipleship programs seem no different than before. Don't some of your Christian friends act the same year after year? Barna notes: "To the naked eye, the thoughts and deeds (and even many of the religious beliefs) of Christians are virtually indistinguishable from those of nonbelievers."[2]

Author Dallas Willard's assessment confirms this belief: "By modest estimate, more than a quarter of the entire population of the United States have professed an evangelical conversion experience. William Iverson wryly observes that 'A pound of meat would surely be affected by a quarter pound of salt.'"[3]

But here is the scary part: Am *I* changing? Maybe I'm the same as I was ten years ago! Perhaps like you, I've attended small-group discipleship studies—I've even led some. I've also read a dozen books on discipleship and attended a dozen weekend seminars. These activities helped me, but maybe I'm included in Barna's sobering statistics?

Christians may talk proudly of no longer getting drunk or cussing, but changes such as these likely occurred during their first year after conversion or rededication. During my first few months as a believer in Christ, my colorful language stopped, and I was noticeably kinder to people. And I felt guilty if I lied. A close friend from back home said, "Okay, something is different about you. What is it?" Not long after, however, my rapid spiritual growth slowed and the changes became far less dramatic.

For most people (myself included) a year or two after becoming a Christian, the Barna stats about lack of transformation begin to set in. The excitement of being in Christ wanes, and zealous new believers experience a drop-off in zeal. They're glad to be saved, and they've eliminated evangelical no-nos from their lifestyle, but spiritual transformation has stopped. The salt no longer affects the meat.

To combat this trend, Christian leaders advocate accountability groups. But even accountability has limitations. A friend named Jeb told me about his accountability group, which formed after several men from his church returned from a conference determined to hold one another accountable for spiritual growth. Jeb said, "For a time, it was great. But then one of the guys moved out of his house—leaving his wife behind—and began living with another woman. He assured us, though, that 'he slept downstairs and she stayed upstairs.' Right. We lovingly confronted him and he sadly admitted that his marriage was dissolving. Moving out 'seemed right,' he'd said.

Jeb was shocked, but continued, "After several unsuccessful confrontations, I figured our errant brother would stop coming to the group. But he told us he enjoyed our fellowship and wanted to continue in Bible study and prayer. He said it was 'good for him.' We didn't know what to do. No one except me wanted to deal honestly with him. The guys felt we shouldn't be too hard on him even though he paid no attention to our repeated admonitions."

Then Jeb started getting animated. "I'm sick of accountability groups. They just don't work."

"What about his church?" I ventured. "Do the pastors know?"

"That's just it," Jeb retorted. "They do know about it, but nobody does anything. I'm quitting the group."

Convinced Jeb's experience was an aberration, I clung to my conviction that accountability is crucial to life change. But my optimism was dashed by a conversation with Bill Thrall of Leadership Catalyst. Bill told me, "Accountability groups are *by themselves* unable to affect deep spiritual growth because they put the resolution of the problem on the person with the problem. But it's too easy to hide. Anyone can hide what he or she doesn't want the group to see. And even if the secret sin is discovered, the group can't help the individual who doesn't want to change."

These and other experiences have convinced me that most Christians are rather naïve about discipleship. In many churches, discipleship is offered as an optional thirteen-week class on Wednesday nights along with other optional classes, such as choir practice or parenting skills. A relatively small percentage of religious types take the course, giving the impression that discipleship is only for those few who are interested in it.

Permit me to declare the obvious: Although attending a discipleship class may be helpful, it does not guarantee change. So how can we be sure—really sure—we're being transformed by Christ?

May I share a secret with you? Concerned that I may not be conforming to the image of Christ (see 2 Corinthians 3:18), I have adopted the following life mission statement:

My mission in life is to daily experience the presence and power of Jesus Christ, becoming ever more conformed to His character and ever more available for joyful service.

I repeat this statement to the Lord each morning. Note the phrase "ever more conformed to His character." Even on my best days, I cannot change myself, no matter how hard I try. Instead, I choose to believe that Christ is transforming me—not just in outward behaviors, but primarily in my values, attitudes, and motives. He's changing all the below-the-surface stuff.

Look at 2 Corinthians 3:18 with fresh eyes: "But we all, with unveiled face beholding as in a mirror the glory of the Lord, are being transformed into the same image from glory to glory, just as from the Lord, the Spirit."

Note the phrase "are being transformed." We needn't struggle to transform ourselves. It happens through the Spirit. The Greek word is *metamorphoo*, and every sixth grader knows metamorphosis describes the process of a caterpillar changing into a beautiful butterfly. But it takes time.

This isn't to say we are passive in this process. Our part, according to the apostle Paul, is to behold the glory of the Lord. I take that to mean beholding in an active, engaged, and awestruck way.

Can you change? Statistics show that if you are over the age of twelve, it is not likely. Thank God—literally—that He he is more powerful than statistics. Paul told the Corinthians, along with you and me, that change is indeed possible. The strange thing is that it may happen without you realizing it, as I learned by a surprise comment from an old friend.

I attended a conference where the speaker gave a stirring talk on the importance of forgiving one another and righting old wrongs. At the time, I was experiencing self-doubt as to whether I was really the man I ought to be. Then in an unexpected move, the speaker gave us thirty minutes to walk around the room to make things right with others and seek resolution for harm done or offense taken.

I was shocked. Those of us in attendance had worked together on and off for years. Should I confess sin to someone? Would someone confront me with some unkind thing I said years ago? I sat anchored to my seat.

Slowly, people began to rise and mill about. There were smiles, tears, and hugs. Taking courage, I arose and wandered the room, apprehensively seeking someone to whom I owed an apology. Then Gloria came directly toward me. She was vivacious with an inviting smile. We had previously been on staff at the same ministry but had not worked together for twelve years. Surely, she didn't have anything to resolve with me!

In a flash, I recalled our days together when I considered her a threat to my leadership, given my youthful insecurity. With her demanding job during the day, ministry groups at night, and imminent marriage plans, Gloria was one who came to tears easily. But I respected her no-nonsense approach to work and ministry. Now, as she drew closer, she caught my eyes and locked in. I prepared to be humbled.

Smiling, she thanked me for the example of godliness I had been to her over the years. In disbelief, I stammered, "But Gloria, I was awfully insecure in those days when we worked together. I know I was insensitive to you."

Her reply floored me: "Oh, Scott, you've changed," she said. "You are not the same person." Then she smiled and went on her way. I just stood there.

The changes she referred to were not the typical new-Christian things like language or moral behavior. She was talking about below-the-surface character issues that are hard to detect and harder to change. Her words that night were a signal that spiritual transformation can happen—even to me!

How about you? Can you change? Yes, but not by self-effort and ardent attempts at behavior modification. "Transformation" is a better way to describe it, and you may not realize it is happening until twelve years later. But you can start today by asking this question: Am I doing *my part* (beholding the glory of the Lord) so that I can become conformed to the image of Christ?

CHAPTER 4

spiritual disciplines: work, work, work

O VER THE YEARS, I HAVE ASKED hundreds of believers about their practice of spiritual disciplines—things like Bible reading, prayer, church attendance. Here are recurring answers:

- "I need to pray more, but I always pray before meals and sometimes while driving to work."
- "I'm pressed for time so I use quick-read devotional booklets with one-sentence prayers at the bottom of each page."
- "We take turns reading Bible stories to the kids at bedtime."
- "It's such a hassle to get everybody ready for church. We enjoy the morning alone as a family more."
- "Solitude? Did you say, 'Solitude'? Hah! I have three kids and a whiny husband."

Many Christians dejectedly admit a guilt-gap between their desire to know God and their consistency in the spiritual disciplines. The disciplines have become "ought-tos" or "I'm going tos." I *ought to* spend more time in Bible study. I'm *going to* pray more often—really.

Living with ought-tos year after year produces a sense of futility and maybe a love-hate attitude toward these wonderful activities. We love the disciplines when we do them and we hate them when we don't.

Let's start over. First, what are the spiritual disciplines? Some call them the "basics," but to most believers they are simply Bible reading, Bible study, prayer, Scripture meditation, church attendance, fellowship with other believers, fasting, and maybe solitude. Perhaps the problem begins with misunderstanding their purpose.

The disciplines are not the end point of the Christian life, but a *means* to intimacy with Christ. Think of them like spokes on a bicycle wheel. Spokes connect the hub of the wheel with the rim. Without spokes, the power generated in the hub cannot travel to the rim. And the rim depends on the spokes to give it shape. Without spokes, the rim is disconnected from the source of power. Spokes are small but crucial connectors. Furthermore, as the wheel spins around, we don't see the spokes but only the rim and the hub. Like spokes, the disciplines do not call attention to themselves.

Knowing the purpose of the disciplines is important, because too many believers evaluate their spiritual maturity based on their "spokes." But if you wanted to buy a new bicycle, you would not base your decision on the spokes! Evaluating my spiritual maturity based primarily on my consistency in the disciplines measures the wrong thing—the means to maturity, not maturity itself.

Besides misunderstanding the purpose of the disciplines, here are two misconceptions about the disciplines that frustrate believers:

1. *Consistency in the disciplines builds immunity to temptation.* The apostle Paul warned against such fallacy. During the first century, Gnostics tried to convince the Colossian believers that spiritual maturity required severe adherence to rules and regulations about what to eat and which holy days to observe (disciplines). Paul warned the Colossians: "These are matters which have, to be sure, the *appearance* of wisdom in self-made religion and self-abasement and severe treatment of the body, but are of *no value against fleshly indulgence*" (2:23, emphasis added).

Obeying rules in our walk with Christ may give an *appearance* of spirituality, but rules have *no value* against fleshly temptation. Think of it: no value! In my early days as a believer, I mistakenly thought that more praying and more Bible study would make my temptations disappear. Wrong.

2. *The disciplines lead to legalism.* The legalistic Gnostics of Colossi were outdone by other church fathers, who went to extreme measures to achieve godliness. They were called "Ascetics." The word *ascetic* comes from the Greek *askesis*, which means "training." A second-century church father, Origen, brilliantly set forth a systematic statement of the faith, but also castrated himself, taking Jesus' words in Matthew 19:12 literally. He thus became an unwitting champion of asceticism.[1]

In AD 423, Simeon the Stylite became renown for living on a pillar platform to display the disciplines of fasting and doing without. According to historian J. D. Douglas, "For 36 years he lived in great austerity on a platform at the top of a pillar, the height of which was gradually increased until it reached 60 feet from the ground. Thousands came to see him and to hear his preaching, with the result that his influence was extensive."[2]

Do the extremes of a few suggest that spiritual disciplines are dangerous? Overreacting, some believers today minimize the importance of the disciplines so they won't become legalistic. I've done it. Frustrated that praying, Bible study, and Scripture memorization didn't make me into a major prophet, I decided to decrease my quiet times, praying, and church involvement. After all, I didn't want to become legalistic. That was unwise.

Author Dallas Willard puts the disciplines in perspective: "A discipline for the spiritual life is, when the dust of history is blown away, nothing but an activity undertaken to bring us into more effective cooperation with Christ and his Kingdom."[3]

There is no definitive list of disciplines—these eight and no more—so I am freed up to ask: What deliberate activities can I do that will draw me into deeper intimacy with Christ?

Rather than be yoked to those disciplines that seem overwhelming, I seek those that energize me while bringing me into the presence of God. For example, I am drawn to intimacy with Christ through watching birds alone in the swamp, recording them on my little list and unhurriedly observing their habits. A deep sense of the power of God envelops me as I walk. Bird-watching and praise of the One who created birds mix into one.

Okay, you may have no interest in watching birds, but can you discover a few practices that bring you into the presence of God. Here are a few more of my freeing disciplines:

- Meditating word by word on one Scripture passage printed on a small card as I drive to work.
- Praying through my do list for the week ahead after a late Sunday afternoon workout at the gym.
- Driving to the prairies east of town to read a Psalm and prompt myself with the question: What can I learn of God by watching Colorado weather?
- Diving into side studies—issues and ideas that normally get overlooked—in my quiet times and lingering in intimacy with Christ in what I discover.
- Physically stopping in the hall to pray for five seconds before going into a meeting.

But success with the disciplines requires more than creativity. A few years ago, I met with four busy Christian leaders at 6:30 on a Tuesday morning at Village Inn restaurant to plan an event. An hour and a half later as we prepared to disband, we opened our calendars for the difficult task of finding an agreeable time to meet again. Someone suggested another early-morning meeting, but a fellow named Jim protested, "Please, not in the early morning."

"Why not?" I said. "It's convenient."

Jim's reply startled me with its simplicity. He said earnestly, "I don't want to lose my early-morning time with the Savior."

Jim wasn't trying to impress. Nor was he just trying to maintain a respectable batting average of quiet times. He simply loves Christ—and it shows all over the place.

Today, I can say that I, too, share Jim's genuine love for meeting with Christ in the morning—not because I *have to*, but because I *want to*. I can say truthfully that my time with the Lord (usually, but not always, in the morning) is the highlight of my day.

So why am I telling you this? It's time to stop dreading the disciplines or considering them "ought-tos." Instead, ask yourself, *What special activities can I deliberately do that will help me become more intimate with Christ?*

Gary Thomas, founder of the Center for Evangelical Spirituality, says it this way: "Whatever it takes, create habits, rituals and practices to intentionally remember God."[4] Whatever it takes! The spiritual disciplines are *that important.* Dive in!

growing in prayer: i've already tried

REALITY TV. I CAN STOMACH ONLY about twenty-five seconds of watching immature people quarrel over who is the least self-centered. And then I start wondering where the camera is and how they fix the lighting and microphone booms while still making the contestants feel "real" enough to cry.

But now imagine that camera crew coming to *your* house to film your prayer times! If they came to film me, viewers would observe me:

- Praying for six seconds before daydreaming about a Peewee baseball game in which I caught an over-the-shoulder line drive and won the game with a last-inning broken-bat single and tipped my hat to the cheering crowd.
- Asking God for a grocery list of stuff as soon as I start my prayer.
- Praying for my staff before mentally shouting at the chief of accounting over the year-end closing problem.
- Getting distracted by the many things that need to be done that day.
- Glancing at the clock and deciding to pray in the car as I dart through traffic.

I would have been kicked off the island! I still occasionally have a "grasshopper mind"—hopping all over the place—but my praying has improved dramatically over time. But I had to get rid of a huge misconception: Prayer doesn't require discipline. True, prayer is often joyful, effortless, and carefree, but other times it requires persistence and perseverance. Sometimes prayer is easy, as natural as breathing, especially during extreme need. In a presentation to a skeptical client, I pray, "Lord, I'm in trouble. Help me survive the Q-and-A session!" That's not work—that's necessity!

Prayer is as close as the Holy Spirit who indwells us. When I drive by an auto accident or hear the wail of an ambulance siren, I pray for the injured. As I think of my son struggling to find a job, I easily pray for him. Praying on the fly is an important byproduct of abiding in Christ, and that's not hard work.

But praying on the fly is not enough. Marriage counselors remind us that communication between husband and wife takes discipline. So does communicating with the One who loves us more than any person on earth. Focused, intentional conversations with the Lord are essential to developing intimacy with Him, and that requires discipline.

My prayer life became more meaningful when I admitted that I needed to add the hard work of discipline. I was not becoming more disciplined as the years went by, and it showed up in my prayer life. Today, because my mind still wanders to Peewee baseball games, I keep my praying short. Better to have three minutes of concentrated focus on God than twenty minutes of daydreaming.

Here is the simple discipline I follow in my devotions: After reading the Scriptures for a few minutes, I open to the daily page in my journal and start immediately with three praises, three thanks, and two confessions:

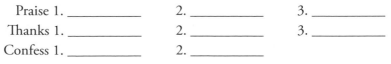

Praise 1. _____   2. _____   3. _____
Thanks 1. _____   2. _____   3. _____
Confess 1. _____   2. _____

Writing them helps if I'm having trouble concentrating. This 3-3-2 practice takes only a couple of minutes, but I often take longer to listen for the voice of God and ponder His character. And here is the exciting part: Though this process begins mechanically, within seconds I am not mechanical! My praying becomes joyful once I get started. And sometimes I praise God for quite a long time. But it begins with discipline.

Why start with praise? That's another observation the TV crew would have made. Besides daydreaming, I drift toward asking — asking God to give me this and help me with that. Disciplining myself *not* to start with my list of requests forces me to think about God rather than my needs or pain. I slow down and consider what I want to say to Him *about Him*. That helps me see things from God's perspective later in the day when things get crazy. Of course, asking has its place, but when I limit my praying to asking, my soul doesn't rise any higher than my own needs and desires.

It's also easy to drift from praising to thanking. Thanking is easier. In thanking, we think about what God has done for us. But in praising we don't think of ourselves at all. Praise is praying the attributes of God back to Him. For example, "As I look out over Pikes Peak this morning, I am reminded that this world of beauty we enjoy was put here by you. I praise you as Creator." After three praises, I thank God for three blessings in the last twenty-four hours. I easily find more than three.

Next, I ask the Lord to bring to mind two personal sins of the past day. I pause a moment. Usually, each thought comes with an internal dialogue (and denial) like this:

"You spent the afternoon stewing about the cash-flow report. You ignored your assistant who needed to talk to you."

"No, I was just planning my presentation; she knows she can interrupt."

Silence. Then I continue, "Okay, I confess that I was stewing. But I'm so scared. Father, I confess. . . ."

Then more silence as I invite the Holy Spirit to speak.

The psalmist understood the need for discipline in praying:

I will give thanks to the LORD with all my heart;
I will tell of all Thy wonders.
I will be glad and exult in Thee;
I will sing praise to Thy name, O Most High. (9:1-2).

Note the four "I wills." The writer of this psalm, like you and me, probably had days when he didn't feel like praising, thanking, or telling of God's wonders. The phrase "I will" describes his *commitment* to do those things even when he didn't particularly feel it.

Thomas More (1478 — 1535), author of *Utopia*, saw the need for a non-wandering mind. He prayed:

Give me thy grace, Good Lord,
To set the world at nought,
To set my mind fast upon thee.[1]

"Fast upon thee." I wish I could tell you that I never daydream or fall asleep in my prayer times. And I wish I didn't drift toward asking so quickly. But I can say that adding discipline to my praying brings joy. Don't be discouraged if you need to find a mechanical way to concentrate during prayer or keep from asking too quickly. Though you may start mechanically, within seconds you'll be sharing intimately in the presence of the King.

misconceptions about temptation

once you've dealt with a particular sin, it's gone forever

YEARS AGO, I WAS AT AN out-of-town meeting where a guy named Ron gave a startling confession. He admitted that for three weeks he had been horribly defeated in his thought-life regarding sexual stuff.

His admission was met with silence.

And more silence.

The ten of us around the table stopped breathing. We thought we were there to discuss committee reports. Ron's confession lay smelly on the table like a three-day-old catfish.

We were stunned. Ron had walked with Christ for twenty-five years and was a leader in his community—and he was always upbeat. But that day, his eyes were misty. We nodded in empathy. I admired his vulnerability.

But his next comment puzzled me: "I thought I would be further along than to still have these struggles. I should be over this by now."

As we sat there, those words—"I should be over this by now"—hung in my mind. Be over what? Do we graduate out of sins like we do a college program? Do we gain victory over a stubborn temptation the way we gain a job promotion? Ron verbalized the unspoken philosophy of sin held by many dedicated believers: "Shouldn't I be victorious by now? Maybe when I turn forty. Or maybe after I'm married. Or when I get appointed to the deacon board at church."

The problem is this unspoken assumption: Our propensity to sin decreases the longer we walk with God. But that's not necessarily so. Years ago, as a new believer struggling with temptations, I was given the "good dog/bad dog" solution for dealing with sin. It goes something like this:

> In every believer's heart are two opposing forces—a good nature and an evil nature. Imagine them as a good dog and a bad dog constantly in battle. To help the good dog win, feed it the disciplines of Bible study, Scripture memory, church attendance, and daily quiet times. At the same time, avoid feeding the bad dog evil thoughts, nasty movies, degrading music, and friends who are poor influences.
>
> As you consistently feed the good dog and starve the bad dog, you will easily defeat the enemy . . . which will become a weak and toothless hound shriveling in a small corner of your heart, never to attack again.

I understood why Ron was crushed. I, too, have faithfully starved the bad dog and fed the good dog. Ron's three-week attack of unrelenting temptation was not supposed to happen—especially since he had committed his sexual life to the Lord long ago.

But the good dog/bad dog doctrine is just plain wrong. True, praying and Bible reading help us become intimate with Christ, and avoiding negative influences is necessary, but these disciplines don't guarantee that our propensity to sin will decrease. Haven't we all suffered defeats in areas we committed to the Lord in absolute sincerity? Our bad dog is not so weak after all. I now visualize the bad dog chained to a strong stake. He still snarls viciously, lunging at me against his chain, but he is a *defeated* foe because of Christ's atoning sacrifice. My enemy can hurt me only when I walk within the length of his chain, within his range to bite me.

We are not getting "better and better." Though we are growing in Christ, we are not fire-walled from "doing the things we used to do" no matter how long we have known the Lord. Longevity-plus-spiritual-disciplines does not weaken the sin nature.

Golfing is a good illustration of this principle. A few years ago while on vacation (with my wife's blessing), I played golf for ten consecutive days—189 holes on the same course. For me, it was a taste of heaven on earth! My early scores of ninety-five, ninety-four, and ninety-nine showed that my old habit of shanking the irons was still with me. In later rounds, by disciplining my swing, my scores dropped to ninety, then eighty-six, and finally, on the last day, eighty-three!

A couple weeks later, with great expectations of shooting seventy-nine, I played the same course. I scored a disappointing ninety-five. I assumed I would start at eighty-three and work down, but my propensity to shank the ball was the same or worse.

Similarly, in the Christian life, we don't inexorably move beyond old, troublesome sins. Previous generations used the phrase "besetting sins" to indicate those issues that continue to plague us. I guess the good news is that we're in good company. Even the apostle Paul's sin nature didn't grow weaker. As he told the believers in Rome, "For the good that I wish, I do not do; but I practice the very evil that I do not wish" (Romans 7:19).

Was Paul an immature believer when he wrote letters to the Roman church? No! Paul wrote those letters on his third missionary journey twenty years after his conversion—that's long enough to get one's act together. I hate to admit it, but I am encouraged by godly Paul confessing his "besetting sins." If he had trouble overcoming obstinate sins, maybe there's hope for me yet.

If the sin nature can't be changed, is Christian growth even possible? Yes, but not by trying to convert the bad dog into an obedient puppy. You can't make your evil nature good. Instead, measure your maturity by how quickly you identify your temptations and bring them to the Lord. For example, having gone down the good dog/bad dog road too many times, here is my prayer in times of temptation: "Lord, I am being tempted to [name the sin]. I enjoy this temptation and I will probably give in. But, deep in my heart I trust you. Right now I submit to God and ask for victory because I am helpless. Amen."

It's not a magic prayer. It comes from James 4:6-7: "But He gives a greater grace. Therefore it says, 'GOD IS OPPOSED TO THE PROUD, BUT GIVES GRACE TO THE HUMBLE.' Submit therefore to God. Resist the devil and he will flee from you."

I used to *resist* without *submitting*. That's dealing with the enemy on my own strength, and that's pride! At that point, God opposes me. Because the evil nature is stronger than my self-effort, winning comes only as I humbly submit to God. That humble submission produces an unexplainable grace that sends the devilish temptation packing. As I humbly pray, I visualize Christ with his arm around my shoulder walking me away from the snarling bad dog straining at his leash.

I'm not getting *better and better*. Instead, I try to be *quicker and quicker* to honestly admit I am toying with temptation and then to humbly surrender to the One who has already provided victory. Spiritual maturity is admitting your helplessness and surrendering immediately. That brings victory. But remember, as in golf, you don't start tomorrow with today's victory!

During that Monday-morning meeting where Ron revealed his struggles, his vulnerability reminded me that I, too, struggle with "besetting sins" and that we never graduate from temptations. Instead of struggling to get *better and better,* it's time to be *quicker and quicker* to humbly submit.

growing christians focus on sinning less

SITTING OVER DESSERT WITH CHRISTIAN FRIENDS years ago, I stumbled into a puzzling issue: Is the goal of the Christian life to reduce sin? Join us at the table. Maggie is telling about her ex-husband, who had pressured her to become a Mormon.

"I was told by Mormon missionaries to pray about whether Joseph Smith, founder of the Mormons, was truly a prophet sent from God," Maggie recalled. "They said confidently that God would reveal it to me through prayer. I prayed each night, but no answer came. Then my Mormon husband told me that if I worked real hard at being godly, I could make it into the 'second level.' But he couldn't tell me *how* godly I'd have to be. It was such pressure."

Then John, who was raised in a reputable evangelical children's home, told a similar story.

"Our church had lots of rules to encourage Christlike living," he said. "We couldn't dance or play cards. When we played the board game Parcheesi, we were not allowed to use the dice that came in the box, but made our own numbers out of cardboard to be drawn out of a sack. The rules were there to protect us. We understood that. But it was a lot of pressure. Our Christian maturity was measured by how well we behaved."

Do you see the similarity? The message is this: Spiritual maturity is measured by external behaviors. To achieve godliness, reduce the sins you commit each day. Many sincere believers would be shocked to know they are trying to achieve godliness the same way sincere Mormons are. How? By "working" on your sin.

I've tried it, too. On a weeklong ministry trip, a friend and I noticed that team members constantly criticized one another. We were guilty as well, so we made a pact not to put people down or make sarcastic comments for the next twenty-four hours. We even prayed about it at bedtime. The next night we talked again. How did we do on our non-sarcasm pact? We were embarrassed. Focusing on eliminating sin had not worked. For an entire day, we were both preoccupied with judgmental thoughts. Even when we held our tongues we "thought it." The more we focused on not sinning, the more we sinned.

About that time, I heard the "canary illustration" from an older man whose gentle, quiet demeanor I admired. It goes like this: Our heart is like a birdcage containing a nasty canary. The canary represents our evil nature and it finds perches on the sides of the cage upon which to rest. Those perches are strongholds of sin in our lives. If we eliminate the perches, the canary has fewer and fewer places on which to alight. It will tire of constantly flying and gradually weakens and dies. The Christian who conscientiously eliminates these "sin perches" can potentially live in a sinless state because the evil nature is powerless.

Honestly, I couldn't identify with the "sinless state" because my heart still had plenty of canary landing strips. Nonetheless, I bought the concept. I was convicted by Romans 13:14: "Make no provision for the flesh in regard to its lusts."

So I worked on removing canary perches. Though I didn't realize it, my unspoken goal was to eliminate sin. Sometimes I'd go for a week with "victory" over a nagging sin. But my perches kept rebuilding themselves. Some sins I thought I'd eliminated were back the next day. I couldn't "defeat" a sin once and for all. My canary wasn't getting tired!

Disappointed, I figured my sin angst would resolve itself when I reached age thirty. Surely, my canary will run out of gas when I'm thirty. But thirty came and went, and now I've concluded that *I* will die before the *canary* dies. Frankly, I have stopped trying to kill it.

Is the goal of the Christian life to become sinless? No. I reject the misconception that reducing sinful behavior day after day causes our godliness quotient to rise. My friends at the dessert get-together worked hard to reduce sin, but it produced more pressure than progress. Keeping external behaviors in line to demonstrate spiritual maturity is a losing game.

I cannot forget an old story about Dawson Trotman, founder of The Navigators. He had just given a sermon in the Great Hall at the Glen Eyrie castle in Colorado Springs. But in the sermon he had been too harsh and he knew it. When he finished, the crowd quickly cleared and Dawson found himself alone in the empty Great Hall. He humbly confessed his sin to the Lord.

As the heartbroken Dawson prepared to leave, a young conferee arrived. He had not heard the speech. Dawson greeted him and discovered he didn't know the Lord. Within the hour Dawson led that newcomer to faith in Christ.

I'm impressed at how quickly Dawson accepted forgiveness and dived back into service. If I had committed a public sin like that, I'd need to do a few days of evangelical penance. But Dawson knew he was a saint who sins rather than a sinner trying desperately to be a sinless saint. He did not mope about having rebuilt a sin perch but chose to immediately return to duty.

It is time we stopped making the reduction of sin our unspoken goal. Something inside us says we should deal with sin issues *first*—and once they are resolved, *then* we can serve Christ. But it doesn't work. Dawson's canary was alive despite his godliness. Even King David, the godly writer of many heartfelt psalms, found that his canary was alive and well in the Bathsheba incident.

Does this excuse sinful behavior? Do we construct runway beacons on our canary landing strips? No, certainly a child molester must get immediate and drastic help. If you're having an affair or stealing from the company, you must stop.

Okay, so why am I telling you this? Too many Christians are disillusioned because they think the focus of the Christian life is to slowly but surely eliminate sin. But can we sin less by focusing on sinning less?

Jesus' famous words about denying self give an important insight: "If anyone wishes to come after Me, let him deny himself, and take up his cross daily, and follow Me" (Luke 9:23).

The verse doesn't end with what not to do. Focusing on denying self puts the attention on me trying desperately not to sin. For example, not that it's a sin, but for now deny yourself the pleasure of thinking about the old Beatles' tune, "We all live in a yellow submarine, a yellow submarine, a yellow submarine." The more we try *not* to focus on it the more we focus on it. The secret is to focus on something else that enables us to move beyond the yellow submarine.

Jesus' words "follow Me" provide the focus of our life in Christ—Him! I deny self best and most effectively when I turn my thoughts to Christ.

What about sin? He empowers you to deal with sin and you will sin less over time. But don't make "sinning less" your top goal. That centers your Christian life on the wrong person.

Is your focus on being sinless? Or sinning less? Or following Christ? Will you admit your canary is not dying?

confessing the visible sin resolves it

D URING MY DAYS OF CAMPUS MINISTRY, I talked with many young men about sexual purity, and I heard versions of the same story over and over. (If your confessions are not in the sexual arena, hang on—there's a point here for you, too.) The scenario went something like this:

> I knew it was wrong to entertain sexual fantasies about women, and I prayed constantly that God would help me overcome it. Going to the library to study created tempting opportunities, but I couldn't stay away. I positioned myself in a secluded carrel area from where I could "study" women across the room.
>
> I pretended to be engrossed in my books, but actually I was engrossed in sexual thoughts. On the way home, I'd stop at the bookstore and buy a "men's magazine." Afterward, I'd feel so guilty that I couldn't concentrate on my studies. I'd cry out to God to forgive me for lusting and for buying the magazines. I'd vow to be a better Christian. But I knew I'd be back the following night. Why wasn't God helping me?

Although you could replace some of the details, this sounds like a classic pattern of addiction:

Adapted from Bill Thrall, Leadership Catalyst Incorporated

- Determination not to sin
- Temptation pressure building
- Accommodation to make it easy to sin
- Giving oneself permission to sin
- Acting out
- Guilt and shame
- Confession

Then determination starts the cycle over again. Before we move from this topic to other temptations, a word of caution.

You might not struggle with sexual temptations, but perhaps you are vulnerable to worry or anger or a critical spirit. Bill Thrall of Leadership Catalyst told me this: "We must not judge as immature or ungodly those who have addictive tendencies to which we are not vulnerable. But at the same time, we hide the sins to which we are vulnerable from the judgment of those very same people."

Back to the library. The young man confesses to buying magazines and lusting. But is there a deeper issue he also ought to confess?

Matthew 5:27-30 helps us delve behind the sinful behavior. This is the famous Jimmy Carter passage of "committing adultery in the heart." (For those too young to remember, former President Carter had the honesty to say that he, like most men, was tempted with sexual lust. As you can imagine, the media had a field day with that admission!) Verses 29 and 30 are puzzling but insightful:

> "And if your right eye makes you stumble, tear it out, and throw it from you; for it is better for you that one of the parts of your body perish, than for your whole body to be thrown into hell. And if your right hand makes you stumble, cut it off."

Does Jesus want us to literally tear out our eyes? Should Jimmy Carter have worn an eye patch? If Jesus is speaking literally, then Lustful Eye Removal (LER) would replace LASIK surgery as a popular medical procedure. Hospitals would advertise it on billboards beside interstate highways! Of course, most of the male doctors doing LERs would be blind!

If Jesus is not literally commanding us to tear out our right eye or cut off our right hand, what's His point? Jesus forces us to address the root problem. Is the eye the problem? Tear it out! Is the hand the problem? Cut it off.

Is it possible that a faint smile crosses Jesus' face as He wryly compels His listeners to discover the source of sexual lust—the mind and heart? He carries His argument to the extreme to force His listeners to address the real issue.

Is buying nasty magazines the sin? Not entirely. The magazines are only the visible outcome of a mindset that says the buyer will find fulfillment and significance by lusting. The real confession ought to go something like this: "Father, I confess that my sin goes deeper than buying nasty magazines. I confess that to feel significant I succumb to the urge to engage in sexual fantasies. I confess my lack of trust in you to satisfy my deepest longings."

Merely confessing the behavior and expecting it not to recur is like cutting off Canadian Thistles in a cow pasture at ground level. For a few days, the pasture looks clean. But soon, the below-ground roots have regrown even tougher thistles.

Now let's apply "true confessions" elsewhere. How about anger? "Lord, I confess I lashed out at my family yesterday." Good start, but the prayer confesses behavior only. It ought to continue: "Lord, I confess yesterday's angry outburst, and I acknowledge the deeper issues that caused it. When I came home after a hard day of board meetings, I was hoping for a big welcome from my family. When they barely greeted me, I felt unappreciated. Feeling hurt, I lost my temper. I confess my self-centered agenda. Help me to be like you—serving rather than wanting to be served."

How about boastful pride? Admitting to God that you boasted is a good start, but it needs to go deeper—perhaps like this: "Lord, I confess that yesterday I succumbed to bragging about my accomplishments to my co-workers. I realize now that I felt insecure. Help me understand that you are my 'Loving Advocate' and that I need not talk about myself so much."

Do you see the difference? Confessing the behavior is only the start. I find it helpful to ask: "Lord, what is it about *you* I don't understand that enflames my vulnerability to this particular temptation?"

Confessing our underlying false beliefs (the real sin) exposes our vulnerable heart to a loving God who desires to give us His grace for the temptation. Then, with God's grace applied to my weakness, temptation's seduction can be broken. The promise in 1 John 1:9 is wonderfully true: "If we confess our sins, He is faithful and righteous to forgive us our sins and to cleanse us from all unrighteousness." Thank God.

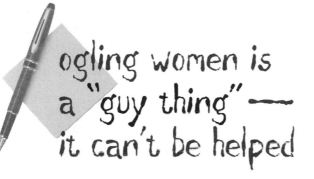

ogling women is a "guy thing" — it can't be helped

I WAS FIFTEEN THE DAY I HIRED out to Old Ben Kennedy to shell corn for $1.25 per hour. When it was lunchtime, we "men" washed up outside in basins with warm soapy water set out by Mrs. Kennedy and Lucy, her pretty fourteen-year-old-assistant.

My eyes wandered repeatedly to the curvaceous Lucy. She had long dark curly hair and full red lips. Though she was only fourteen, she had "developed early," as puberty was properly described in Plymouth County.

Inside the house, it was sweaty and crowded as eight of us squeezed around the dining room table. Though the ladies of Plymouth County usually did not eat with the men because of limited table space, this day both Lucy and Mrs. Kennedy joined us—as it should be, I thought.

Lucy was seated three places to my left and slightly across the table. She was wearing a short-sleeved cotton sweater with slightly bulging buttons. I hoped she didn't notice me sneaking glances. She was gorgeous. I couldn't take my eyes off her. I planned to ask her to marry me right after lunch.

Then it happened. When the mashed potatoes were passed, Lucy politely declined. Mrs. Kennedy nonchalantly asked if Lucy was "watching her figure."

Oops! Sudden silence. All conversations stopped. Everyone's eyes went to Lucy—an innocent Delilah in a roomful of Samsons. Mrs. Kennedy's humble attempt at humor backfired. Someone needed to say something.

It was Old Ben. "Lucy, you don't need to watch your figure—the rest of us will watch it for you!" The table erupted with laughter. Even Lucy laughed and blushed. I blushed, too . . . and I lost some innocence.

Many years have passed since I shelled corn at Ben Kennedy's, but the observation I made that day is still true. Advice columnist Cheryl Lavin of the *Chicago Tribune* captured it this way:

Fish gotta swim, birds gotta fly,
Men gotta look at pretty women till they die.

Men, even married men, "look" at women. Some stare discreetly behind dark glasses. Some dart their eyes furtively. Others blatantly turn their heads 360 degrees like owls to follow well-formed legs. But the thing that bothers me most is that believers are guilty of it, too.

A hotel manager told me he made more money on porno TV rentals at Christian conventions than from any other group. *Internet Filter Review* reports that 53 percent of the constituents of a major ministry view pornography during an average week. Even as fellow believers sit across from me at restaurants telling me about their prayer lives, I have noted their eyes riveted to the curves of attractive waitresses.

This is an area where believers could set the standard for society, but Christian men seem to have bought into the "married man's ogling guideline," which might be stated: "It's okay to window shop as long as you don't touch the merchandise."

Window shopping? Pornography on the Internet grosses more

money than all professional sports combined.[1] And the largest consumer group of Internet pornography is twelve- to seventeen-year-olds.[2] *Business Week* said that 44 percent of workers with an Internet connection visited an X-rated website in March 2004.[3]

Some say women are to blame. Yes, some women get a self-esteem boost by flaunting their attractiveness before men. But men lust after fully clothed women, too. The Taliban covered women from head to toe with the burka to "protect" them. But does covering women stop male lusting?

What about women lusting after men? In a recent TV commercial, a group of young women are peering excitedly out a window at a young "hunk" working shirtless on a street crew below. But that is not nearly as common as men eying women. God has made women more responsive to emotions and touch than what they see. A university co-ed told me that in her opinion, "When women see a 'hunk,' we say to ourselves, *I bet he's nice!*"

Certainly, women can fantasize, too, but their fantasies are not likely to be erotic so much as romantic — being treated "nice" by a good-looking man.

Are we powerless to stop? Must we fantasize? Three suggestions are in order:

1. Realize that mental adultery is a sin against a holy God and is recorded on "Heaven's Big Board." Jesus said in Matthew 5 that while enjoying a little opposite-sex browsing, a man "has committed adultery with her already." It's hard to ignore that.
2. Understand that the *temptation* is not the sin. When a curvaceous "Lucy" passes your way, thank God for making such a beautiful creature. But before you take a second look . . .
3. Surrender the temptation to the Lord immediately. Tell Him you are overwhelmed by this beautiful woman He created. Humbly confess that you are powerless and ask

for strength to be pure. And then by His grace think about something else.

We all need to follow the commitment of the suffering servant Job in the Old Testament, who said: "I have made a covenant with my eyes; how then could I gaze at a virgin?" (31:1). How indeed? Job had already decided what he would do when curvaceous Lucys came his way.

Please pass the potatoes.

you'll always be a people-pleaser

I HAVE A CONFESSION. PEOPLE-PLEASING has been my biggest problem. I'm embarrassed to tell you the desperate stuff I've done to win approval. Just a few examples:

- Speaking up at meetings only when I had a well-rehearsed comment sure to impress.
- Not speaking up at meetings for fear I would not impress.
- Exaggerating or tossing powerful phrases into my conversations to show how spiritual I was. For example: "I went for a three-mile run this morning—after my six o'clock quiet time."
- Blaming others to save face. "I'm sorry, Mr. O'Brien, your ad didn't run because the boys in the back shop goofed."

My most memorable people-pleasing performance came the day I had lunch with a godly veteran missionary. Also at the table were my Bible study leader and his nicely coiffed fiancé. I was a new believer, eager to impress. During dessert, I volunteered to bring coffee to our table. At the coffee station, I smugly imagined what my three tablemates might be saying about my servant spirit.

I soon returned with three steaming cups of coffee, two in one hand, my fingers woven through the coffee mug rings. I smiled, anticipating their warm expressions of thanks sure to come in the next five seconds. That's when I accidentally poured steaming coffee down the back of the beautiful fiancé. She screamed like a Baptist at a tattoo parlor, and two hundred surprised diners looked our way. I made an impression all right!

Though that embarrassing scene helped me realize how deeply I longed to impress others, I didn't know how to stop. Focusing on trying to get over it made me even more aware of my pretentious motives. The turning point came the day I was accidentally locked out of our home in Iowa City. While I waited for my wife to return, I wandered into the Lutheran church across the street.

I had been thinking about the subject of "identity" and guessed that my people-pleasing tendency was rooted in how I viewed myself. In the afternoon sunlight of a stained-glass window, I pulled out my pocket New Testament and glanced over 1 Corinthians 4. Paul saw his identity as a *servant* of Christ and a *steward* of the mysteries of God. Good start.

Then I noticed verse three: "But to me it is a *very small thing* that I should be examined by you" (emphasis added).

"Very small thing!" Had I been writing the Corinthians, I would have said, "It is a *very large thing* that I should be examined by you. Your opinion means everything."

My conscience already worked overtime telling me that the opinion of others shouldn't be so important, but Paul said plainly that others' opinions of him were "a very small thing." What a contrast!

Then the last six words of verse three floored me. Paul said, "I do not even examine myself." Wait a minute! Aren't we supposed to examine ourselves? He explains it in verse four: "I am conscious of nothing against myself, yet I am not by this acquitted; but the one who examines me is the Lord."

Until that moment, I assumed that my opinions of myself were accurate. But were they?

For example, in a team meeting, we were asked to identify our strengths and weaknesses. To my surprise, when I mentioned my strengths, no one nodded in agreement. And when I listed my weaknesses, several team members frowned. Finally, someone said, "Scott, those things you put down as weaknesses are really strengths."

Befuddled, I countered, "But I don't feel good at them."

"Well, you are," another person said. And the group agreed.

"So what about the things I listed as strengths?" I queried.

No one spoke. No one even looked at me. I got the message. My opinion of myself was faulty. I could finally agree with Paul: It is the Lord's job to examine us—accurately.

Back to verse four: Paul said he was conscious of nothing against him. In my people-pleasing days, I frequently sought out friends and co-workers to see if I had offended them. They thanked me for inquiring, but usually no one had an offense to resolve. Why did I go to them so often? Because I got my identity from people liking me. But Paul said, "I am not by this acquitted." It finally made sense. I was equating people liking me with pleasing God. My focus was on *others'* opinions. Do my co-workers like me? Do my fellow church members accept me? Am I offending the boss? I was more concerned with their opinion than God's. People were big and God was little.

I was playing to an audience of hundreds, each with different opinions. No wonder I was always tired.

Paul's next statement also helped me with something I didn't want help with—a critical spirit! He said, "Therefore do not go on passing judgment before the time, but wait until the Lord comes who will both bring to light the things hidden in the darkness" (1 Corinthians 4:5).

People-pleasers are critical people—especially with those they find hard to please. For example, if I long for you to approve of me and you don't, then I have no choice but to criticize you. But Paul says to wait for the Lord to be the chief critic. That is His job, not mine.

The last clause of verse five brings us to the audience of one: "Then each man's praise will come to him from God." Unlike people, God can be pleased. He's not fickle; He doesn't change his opinion on what is "in" or "out." And when I fail, His love makes me want to trust Him still more.

I walked out of that Lutheran church still a people-pleaser, but I had hope that I could change. How? Not by trying harder, but by thinking differently. I prayed over this passage every day for six weeks — some days in depth and some days just mentioning it in passing. And for a while, my people-pleasing tendencies worsened as I caught myself doing it more. But each time, I confessed and reminded myself I had but "One" to please and He loved me.

I can say today that people-pleasing is no longer a major issue for me. Sure, my motives are never 100 percent perfect, and I love compliments, but others' approval no longer means life and death. And I'm much less critical.

In fact, today I want to please others, not to boost my ego, but to see others helped by my words or actions simply because it is right. I am free to serve others for their benefit, not mine.

Everyone is tempted to impress. It doesn't go away by itself. Maybe you could find new freedom from spending a few days meditating on 1 Corinthians 4:1-5. Write it out in your own words — even if you're not in a Lutheran church.

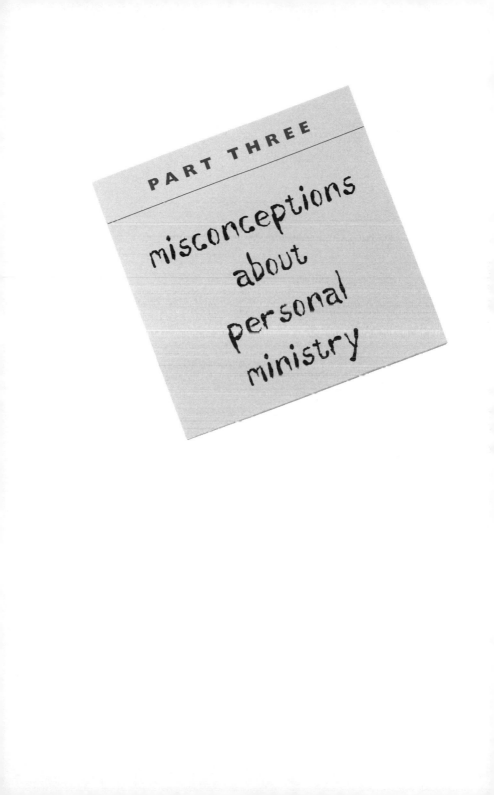

PART THREE

misconceptions
about
personal
ministry

CHAPTER 11

only your spiritual service makes a difference in the world

I F YOU ARE YOUNGER THAN, SAY, thirty-five years old, you may not "get" this chapter. Sometimes in the middle of the night when I get up to go to the bathroom (already those under thirty-five aren't getting it), a discouraging thought hits me: *Is my so-called Christian life making a difference?*

Perhaps in the middle of the night when my defenses are down, I see life more pessimistically—or maybe more accurately! Suddenly, I have questions:

- Do my hours at the office each week help to resolve the *big issues* in the world—starving kids in Africa, child neglect and abuse, poverty, the spread of AIDS, and so on?
- Are the people in my Bible study group being transformed, or are we just sharing the same old problems week after week?
- Was it worth all the time to establish programs at work when young people with pierced body parts whose favorite word is "dude" are dismantling them?
- What about those once-in-a-lifetime vacations I've dreamed of? Will I ever get to enjoy them (even once in a lifetime)?

This popular poem, often found hanging in church basements or soup kitchens, adds to my guilt:

Only one life, twill soon be past.
Only what's done for Christ will last.
　—Author unknown

We give many hours to mundane tasks that don't make a difference—or so it seems. For example, I spent sixty precious minutes recently trying to get the wand on my PDA to talk to my keyboard. Last week, a young mother told me, "I do nothing but fix juice for preschoolers." Significant?

Telling ourselves, "Our efforts are bearing fruit—we just can't see it," seems as shallow as the cliché, "Just trust the Lord." Maybe I should stop drinking liquids after 6:00 p.m., so I'll stop having these midnight fits of self-doubt!

Let's face it, history books will not devote much space to your accomplishments or mine, but does that mean we are not fruitful? An insight is found in an overlooked passage from 1 Corinthians 3, where Paul says that we build upon the foundation of Christ either with "gold, silver, precious stones" or "wood, hay, and straw." Each believer's work will be tested with fire. The wood, hay, and straw burn, but gold, silver, and precious stones *remain.*

In Paul's day, precious metals and stones were used to decorate magnificent buildings, like Herod's temple in Jerusalem. By contrast, ordinary homes were built of wood, dried grass mixed with mud, and thatched straw or stalks for the roof.[1] Obviously, these homes would be quickly consumed in a fire.

Similarly, as we build on the foundation of Christ, we sometimes put in precious non-combustible stones, and sometimes we contribute easily consumed thatched straw. The "fire" is not the fire of hell; salvation is not at stake but rather our service to Christ.

What service? Sunday school teaching? How many souls we saved? How much money we gave? What about "secular" stuff like trying to figure out your PDA? Both! Is Christ interested only in your "church work"? That divides life into sacred and secular and implies that your non-church activities don't matter.

I love the view that the famous violin maker Antonio Stradivari (1644—1737) had about his "secular" profession. He said, "For while God gives them [musicians] skill, I give them instruments to play upon, God choosing me to help Him. . . . He could not make Antonio Stradivari's violins without Antonio."[2]

Cannot all of life be service to Him? He cares about all you do—whether it's violins or PDAs. When done in His power and by His grace, you build with precious stones. I am saddened by believers with so-called "secular" jobs who think they are "not in ministry."

In the middle of the night, I must honestly confess that some of my work is self-centered and will not survive the wood, hay, and straw burn-off! But also, some of what I do, whether in the church or on the job, *will* remain. Yes, I am producing something lasting!

Another insight is found in John 15:16: "You did not choose Me, but I chose you, and appointed you, that you should go and bear fruit, and that your fruit should remain, that whatever you ask of the Father in My name, He may give to you."

Notice the second *that*: "that your fruit should remain. . ."

If Jesus intends my fruit to "remain," why am I whining about not making a difference? Why not *choose to believe* my fruit will remain whether I see it or not? Wanting to see immediate results wrongly convinces us we are insignificant.

A friend of mine recently told me about his autistic grandson. This sweet-spirited four-year-old melts hearts with his unabashed acceptance of whoever happens to be in the room. Though severely speech-delayed, he has deeply affected his whole family. This autistic child is having a ministry of gold, silver, and precious stones.

I also think about my friend, Kathy, and her husband, who received several anonymous cash gifts a few years ago when they were going through tough times. They were grateful to their unknown benefactor but didn't know whom to thank. Today, out of appreciation, they send anonymous gifts to others in need. That anonymous donor does not know the blessing those gifts brought nor about Jim and Kathy's continuing "ministry" to others. That donor built with noncombustible precious stones and will see the multiplied impact on Burn-off Day.

At the end of his first letter to the Corinthians, Paul included this reminder in 15:58: "Therefore, my beloved brethren, be steadfast, immovable, always abounding in the work of the Lord, knowing that your toil is not in vain in the Lord."

"Abounding in the work of the Lord" is more than teaching Sunday school. Whatever you do "in the Lord" is not in vain. The next time I'm up in the middle of the night, I'll choose to believe my life is making a difference. How about you?

CHAPTER 12

to spread the gospel, you must be eloquent

FELT TRAPPED. I WAS PLASTERED against a vinyl-backed booth in the Holiday Inn restaurant in Pierre, South Dakota, having breakfast with the chief of scouting for the Baltimore Orioles. Sitting across from me was his attractive wife. On my left was another Orioles scout. I was hemmed in by three beautiful and influential people—people who could dramatically alter my future.

They had come to South Dakota to see me pitch the night before. Chatting for a few minutes before the game, the chief scout had treated me with courtesy and respect. I liked him, and I desperately wanted him to like me. The scout had stationed himself directly behind home plate so he could gauge my pitching prowess: the movement of my fast ball, the break of my curve, the sharpness of my slider, and the deceptiveness of my changeup. My mind raced as I imagined the superlatives he would give at breakfast the next morning: "We've got a hot prospect here! The Orioles scored when they drafted this left-handed flamethrower!"

As it turned out, I didn't pitch well. Eager to impress, I threw extra hard. That may sound good, but when a fastball pitcher presses too much, the ball doesn't tail in or out as well. I lasted only three innings.

So there we were at the Holiday Inn, and I was nervous. Really nervous. The chief scout—like all baseball scouts, it seems—had shaved that morning with military precision. I brushed my hand against my face hoping not to find straw.

Furthermore, his wife was a knockout. Thick, black hair, perfectly clear skin, and shining eyes. When she smiled, I felt like she was staring into my soul. Her husband introduced her as an "entertainer."

The other scout was older, also clean-shaven, and eager to get me signed. Despite my poor showing the evening before, he saw something he liked—raw potential that could be cultivated. He said the Orioles would pay for my college education if I signed that day to play with the club's "A" league affiliate at Stockton, California.

But I knew that if he offered me a contract with the Orioles, I'd have to explain why I couldn't accept it. And that was why I felt so nervous. Telling the truth might mean I'd have to share my faith. At that moment, I thought I heard ominous music swelling to a crescendo and a coyote howling in the distance.

You see, the truth was that I had enrolled at Maranatha Bible Camp in Nebraska for the remainder of the summer. After breakfast, I would load my family into our '57 Chevy to drive to North Platte. I wasn't quitting baseball; I was taking time off to receive "faith training"—how to better know Christ and to make Him known.

When the scout pressed me to reveal my thoughts about signing a contract, I told him my plans to attend the camp. I mentioned the name, but I stopped short of giving details.

Then came the dreaded follow-up question from the scout: "Why would anyone want to go to Bible camp when they could sign with the Baltimore Orioles?" I panicked. The beautiful entertainer looked at me curiously with her sparkling eyes. Clean-shaven chief scout gazed thoughtfully at me. The scout pressing me to sign fiddled with his coffee cup. They all seemed so cool. And I felt so uncool. And I really, really wanted them to like me.

Silence. An ice age passed. *Just tell the truth!* I urged myself.

But they'll think I'm stupid, I reasoned.

Then I heard a voice smugly say, "I'm going to Bible camp because everyone needs a well-rounded education." More silence. Even as I'd said the words, I knew they didn't ring true. All three of them stared at me.

I forgot who spoke next, but it was awkward. We parted ways without a signed contract.

On the five-hour drive to North Platte, I had plenty of time to think about my great chickening out of a God-given opportunity to discuss my faith in Jesus with a captive audience of three curious people. Why had I avoided revealing the whole truth? Fear. I was afraid they wouldn't like me.

The words of the apostle Paul came to mind many times during that drive: "For I am not ashamed of the gospel, for it is the power of God for salvation to everyone who believes, to the Jew first and also to the Greek. For in it the righteousness of God is revealed" (Romans 1:16-17). The phrase "ashamed of the gospel" rang in my ears over and over. And because I was ashamed, I failed to be authentic. I was so broken that six weeks later I wrote the chief scout a long letter confessing the real reason I went to Bible camp. He wrote a warm letter back, intrigued by my faith in Christ.

I learned a valuable lesson from that chickening-out episode at the Holiday Inn. I got more respect by being honest in my follow-up letter than I did by trying to get the Orioles representatives to like me—and shading the truth to make it sound more palatable! More importantly, the gospel got more respect, too.

In retrospect, I realize I had overlooked the second phrase in Romans 1:16: "For [the gospel] is the power of God." I didn't understand how powerful the gospel is. I mistakenly thought that evangelism was about *me.* In the simple story of the Good News lies great power, for it reveals the righteousness of God.

I wish I could tell you that since the Holiday Inn cop-out, I never again chickened out of an opportunity to share my faith. The truth is, wanting nonbelievers to like me runs deep. However, that breakfast meeting in Pierre was a turning point. That was the day I determined to trust Christ for courage to be honest and authentic. And that removed tons of pressure about personal evangelism. It's not about me. It's about letting the gospel be the gospel, with all its power to change lives.

How about you? Do you ever chicken out of opportunities to talk about Christ? Of course, you do! You probably have your own "trapped at the Holiday Inn" story.

So why have I told you this story? First, to encourage you that you are not the only one who has chickened out. Second, to remind you that you needn't be eloquent or persuasive with nonbelievers, because it is the gospel that is the power of God—not you. Your job is to be authentic and tell the truth. God's job is to bring people to Himself.

sharing your faith will always be an awkward "have-to"

According to pollster George Barna, 1 percent of Christians believe they have the "gift" of evangelism.[1] As for me, I'm among the 99 percent who believe they don't! I cannot imitate those gifted believers who lead strangers to Christ on airplanes and elevators. I am more like the Yukon River of Alaska—frozen at the mouth.

Though I'm not among the gifted 1 percent, today I enjoy evangelism—but only because I've jettisoned two huge misconceptions. Before that, I was doing all the wrong things in trying to share my faith, such as:

Too much, too soon . . . like the time I asked a guy I'd met only once to join an early-morning "Skeptic's Bible Study" without knowing his spiritual history. He came once but never returned my phone calls after that.

Too little, too late . . . like with Juan, who was HIV-positive. We were friends for more than three years, but to avoid being perceived as pushy I postponed inviting him to read the Bible with me. Finally, we did start to read together, and he liked it. But then he suddenly and unexpectedly returned to Puerto Rico, where he died a year later.

Too artificial, too hurried . . . like the many times I've felt guilty if I didn't quickly and artificially steer the conversation to the gospel.

Famous evangelists were my models. Though I wouldn't have admitted it, I was disappointed if I couldn't convince someone to listen intently, answer their questions cogently, recall Bible verses instantaneously, explain concepts persuasively, and press for a decision with urgency. And all of this, I believed, should happen within an hour! I thought I had to take people from agnostic to convert in sixty minutes. Hey, if I knew all the answers, it shouldn't take longer than that. But, of course, that was mistake #1: Viewing evangelism as an *event* rather than a *process*.

I should have realized my error by examining my own spiritual journey. I didn't "pray the prayer" the first time I heard the gospel. It was a process of personal discovery as the Hound of Heaven pursued me.

First, I was raised in a stable home with caring parents. Then a Sunday school teacher taught me stories about Jesus. At the same time, I noticed a painting of Jesus knocking at a door that hung in the dank basement of our country church. When I was a teen, I "went forward" at an evangelistic meeting and stopped cussing for a couple days thereafter. Then our pastor met with several of us teens individually, and he prayed a prayer with me. At college I saw posters for Christian ministries and determined to avoid them. "Do-gooders," I sniffed.

During this time, I managed to read the Bible occasionally. When Jesus said in Matthew 12 that the "Queen of the South" would "rise up," I figured I'd marry a girl from the South. Well, at least I was trying to apply Scripture to my own life.

Then I met Bob, who invited me to join a weekly Bible study, which I sometimes skipped. Seven months later at a Christian conference, I heard a businessman quote Revelation 3:20 about Jesus standing at the door knocking. I reflected back to the painting I'd seen in the church basement. That day I opened the door to Jesus in a simple prayer.

I share these details to illustrate that the "event" of my trusting Christ was preceded by a long "process" involving people, a painting, and posters.

Jesus says in Matthew 13:19: "When anyone hears the word of the kingdom, and does not understand it, the evil one comes and snatches away what has been sown in his heart." The word *understand* implies a process. Sometimes the lightbulb of truth goes on immediately, but most often it's on a dimmer switch that increases the light slowly and gradually.

One time, I had a wonderful gospel encounter with a fellow student who seemed prepared by God to meet Christ. He listened attentively and read with interest the Bible verses we looked up. Then he prayed to receive Christ . . . all in sixty minutes. A big smile crossed his face. We agreed to meet the next day to talk further, but when I arrived I found only a note explaining that he had talked to his pastor and said he felt misled. He left the Bible I had given him.

Sure, it was an obvious attack of the enemy, but it also shows he did not *understand* enough about Christ to hold the weight of his decision. I wish now that instead of asking him for a decision, I'd have simply invited him to explore and discuss some Scriptures together. Who knows what might have happened?

If George Barna's 1 percent figure is correct, then why would Jesus knowingly give the Great Commission to the other 99 percent of us who are not evangelists? Rather than trying to copy the 1 percent, I focus on being a faithful link in the chain. I'm content to "sow" and be thankful for those few gifted people who "reap" the results of a long process toward salvation.

I stumbled onto misconception #2 the day I found the phrase in 2 Corinthians 2:14 that says God reveals "through us the sweet aroma of the knowledge of Him in every place." The following verse says we are a "fragrance of Christ." Believers give off an odor — not a physical body scent (usually), but the aroma of God wherever we go. We don't *work* at giving off this aroma any more than we work at giving off the aroma of perfume or morning aftershave.

My misconception? Working too hard at being "odiferous." I thought it all depended on me. In my head, I knew it depended on God, but my actions showed I felt pressure to "make something happen." I was too pushy, too artificial, and too uptight.

Last September, an electrician was at our house installing new kitchen lights. Both my wife and I commented that he must be a believer, though he uttered not one religious word and had no religious bumper sticker on his truck. His gentleness, honesty, and unexpected offer to clean up drywall dust were the only clues we had. Before he departed, we got to talking and, sure enough, he was a believer. We smelled the aroma!

Now one caution: Many Yukon River Christians take these two misconceptions to imply that they don't have to open their mouths. Their motto is: "Share the gospel, and if necessary use words." That's a great principle, but not entirely complete. I asked the late Navigator missionary and author Leroy Eims about that statement, which is attributed to Saint Francis of Assisi. Leroy's response gave balance: "Sooner or later, it *will* take words."

I am not uptight about evangelism today, because I've stopped trying to get people to pray the sinner's prayer in sixty minutes. Instead, I see myself as an "aromatic" part of the process of deepening people's understanding of Jesus. The Hound of Heaven pursues them, and though I don't have the gift of evangelism, I am an important player on the Body of Christ team. Urgency? Yes. Pressure? No. I give off an aroma simply by being in Christ! And so do you.

avoid worldliness — stay in the holy huddle

NOT LONG AGO, MY WIFE, ALMA, and I were in the Midwest to attend a thirty-year wedding anniversary party of two delightful friends. They are terrific Christians and lots of fun. Many cars were parked outside their nicely decorated home. Alma and I wondered what kind of people would show up, and we hoped we would fit in. Our curiosity was soon satisfied as we were introduced first to a friend from their church, then another friend from their church, then another friend from their church. You get the idea.

Of the fifty-three partygoers, forty-seven were from our friends' church. We had a wonderful time mingling and meeting new people, but Alma and I both had a nagging feeling as we left the party. After some discussion, we put our fingers on it—and it's a situation common to many believers. Like carbon monoxide, we can't see or smell it, but without it our Christian lives shrivel. What is missing?

- Love for one another?
- Having fun together?
- Church attendance?
- Service?
- Commitment to Christ?

None of the above. The missing link is deliberately spending time with nonbelievers. To the credit of the anniversary couple, a few of the party revelers were not from their church. But wouldn't it have been great to have more nonbelievers at their party—to get acquainted with Christians and to participate in a celebration of a thirty-year marriage centered on Christ?

It's not hard to see that we believers prefer the company of people like us. We attend Bible studies with Christians only, we eat out with believers, we play golf with believers, and we go to movies with believers. Many Christians rarely, if ever, have into their home people outside the "family of faith." Furthermore, we seek out Christian hairdressers, Christian doctors, Christian stockbrokers, and Christian plumbers. In some cities, you can find directories of Christian businesses and tradespeople.

A few years ago, I received a surprise about evangelicals' attitudes toward nonbelievers. I was teaching an evangelism class for young married couples at our church—dedicated believers upon whom strong churches are built. After a couple weeks of laying the biblical groundwork, I passed out index cards and gave this assignment: "List the names of nonbelieving friends you could invite to your home for a meal. Your goal is not to spring the gospel on them, but just to enjoy a nice evening together."

The couples just stared at me. I repeated the question. They studied the index cards intently, as if names would magically appear from the cotton fibers. Slowly, a few picked up their pens and doodled on the cards. Embarrassed, I ventured, "Is this a difficult question?"

A fellow named Ted broke the silence. "Scott, we have non-Christian *acquaintances*, but we don't have non-Christian *friends*," he explained. "And especially none we want around our homes."

Relieved, other members looked up and nodded.

Startled, I said, "But you work with nonbelievers every day. You're around them all the time!"

Ted didn't budge. "But they are not our friends. And besides, what if they cussed or smoked around our kids?"

One by one, other class members revealed their reticence to associate with nonbelievers. And it wasn't merely a preference — there was a strong bias to avoid nonbelievers.

Martin Marty, theologian and editor of the publication *Context,* says that two main cultures exist side by side in America — evangelicals and everybody else. He says both are so separate that "neither acts as if the other exists" (except, of course, if there's a protest involving a moral issue or hotly debated legislation).

So is this a bad thing? Doesn't 2 Corinthians 6:17 admonish us to "come out from their midst and be separate"? The apostle Paul told us not to be "conformed to this world" (Romans 12:2). And 1 John 2:15 says "Do not love the world." Fair enough, these are prudent precautions. But understand what I'm saying. Although we must be discerning about when, where, and how we associate with nonbelievers — especially if we fear our morals, or the morals of our children, will be compromised. But so many Christians today simply retreat within the safety and security of the Christian castle. Do these biblical warnings really mean we are to be isolated — Seinfeld-like "Bubble Boy Christians" sealed in plastic wrap to avoid a hostile society?

Many dedicated believers have not discovered the refreshing exhortation in 1 Corinthians 5:9-11:

I wrote you in my letter not to associate with immoral people;
I did not at all mean with the immoral people of this world, or
with the covetous and swindlers, or with idolaters; for then you
would have to go out of the world.

But actually, I wrote to you not to associate with any so-
called brother if he is an immoral person.

Paul reminds us not to abandon nonbelievers by sealing ourselves off from the world — otherwise, we would have to leave the planet. Instead, we are to disassociate with so-called *believers who are immoral.*

The Greek word translated *associate* is *sunanamignumi*. *Sunana* means "with" or "up," and *mignumi* means to "mingle."

Jesus mingled! Luke 15:2 reports that the Pharisees grumbled at Jesus for eating with sinners. In Mark 2:15-17, we read that He is criticized for eating and drinking with tax collectors and sinners. Jesus had a reputation for hanging out with the unconverted.

I have found that hanging out with nonbelievers exhilarates my walk with Christ. When not involved with the lost, I focus on my job, my family, my Christian friends, my green grass, church politics, and sometimes my golf score. But when I am personally involved with nonbelieving people, my prayer life takes on new vitality as I plead for the spiritual lives of those I have come to care about. I also feel like I experience God more—like I'm more in step with God's agenda.

It is time for us believers to break out of our holy huddles and hang out with nonbelievers. *Mingle!* Salt doesn't do much in the shaker! We must make a deliberate decision to socialize with and befriend people who don't share our beliefs. Won't nonbelievers come to our Christian circles if we just invite them and have good snacks? Well, some might risk it. But the holy huddle looks scary from the sidelines. At least 50 percent of America did not attend a religious service last weekend, and they do not intend to anytime soon.

Start by praying for God to bring two nonbelieving friends across your path this week. When they come, take time with them—not to ambush them with the gospel, but simply to engage in conversation. Build a friendship. Take them to lunch. Invite them to dinner on a Friday night. As the friendship grows, it will be impossible to avoid talking about spiritual issues.

One last thought on this point: In Jesus' final prayer the night before He was crucified, He prayed to the Father about His followers, saying, "I also have sent them into the world" (John 17:18). Let's go.

PART FOUR

misconceptions
about
emotional
health

CHAPTER 15

committed christians
don't get discouraged

PERHAPS YOU'VE SUNG THE OLD HYMN, "What a Friend We Have
in Jesus." It contains these famous lines:

Are we weak and heavy laden? Cumbered with a load of care?
We should *never be discouraged*, take it to the Lord in prayer.

Hmm. *Never be discouraged?* I wince as I sing this hymn, because
I *do* get discouraged. Maybe you do, too. So did the psalmist who
wrote, "Why are you in despair, O my soul? And why have you become
disturbed within me?" (42:5).

Why, indeed? I see many believers today stuck in the paralysis of
discouragement—like a deer in the headlights. Instead of addressing
root causes, they fumble with coping strategies. Recognize any?

- Escape: overeating, oversleeping, oversexing, overdrinking,
  watching hours of Dr. Phil, or fixating on my vacation coming
  up in forty-nine short weeks.
- Denial: ignoring my feelings and working still harder (which
  could be another form of escape).

- Self-pity and complaining: feeling sorry for myself inwardly or out loud.
- Retreat into hurt: feeling sorry for myself in seclusion.
- Anger or striking out: seeking to regain the illusion of control.

I wonder if we could handle discouragement more victoriously if we understood the process. Long ago a veteran missionary shared with me the Four Ds of Discouragement. I pass them on to you.

Disappointment. It is impossible to be discouraged without a precipitating disappointment, large or small. Somewhere an expectation has been dashed.

Doubt. After disappointment comes self-doubt, looking for explanations to make sense of the disappointment. For example, you were hoping for a hefty pay raise after a year of hard work, but you received the standard cost-of-living increase—same as the slackers! You're disappointed. Now comes self-doubt. "Am I being passed over? Am I liked?"

Disillusionment. Here, self-doubt morphs into subjective speculations, such as blaming others, unrealistically assessing my abilities, and concluding life would be better in Vegas. To continue the pay raise scenario: "I'll bet my supervisor hates me. The big boss hates me, too. That plaque I got at the Christmas party was a ruse. They want to get rid of me, and they always have. I'll probably have to give my parking space to 'Nitwit Bob' in corporate. I'll lose my corner office and have to work in a three-by-six-foot cubicle or maybe out of the trunk of my car. No more cafeteria privileges. It's minced ham sandwiches in the parking lot! This job sucks. I'm going to Vegas."

Even the psalmist faced disillusionment. In Psalm 69:4, the writer moans, "Those who hate me without cause are more than the hairs of my head." The Trichological Society (that's right, trichological—hair-like), which keeps track of such things, says human hair counts run from 50,000 to 146,000. David was convinced his enemies were even more!

Discouragement. The unrealistic speculations of disillusionment soon lead to full-fledged discouragement, in which we resort to our coping mechanisms (daydreaming about Las Vegas) . . . which usually leads to guilt . . . which leads to shame and even greater discouragement.

Many Christians needlessly wander in the wilderness of discouragement because they haven't identified where they are in the Four-D process. I'll show you what I mean.

First, identify your *disappointment*. That's not always easy. For example, I spent one Friday night and all day Saturday acting grouchy, but I didn't know why until I finally slowed down enough to remember that my assistant had frowned at me Friday at 5:00 p.m. as I left the office. I took her frown home with me, assuming she was disgruntled.

Doubt crept in: "You're not a good boss. You should have more thoroughly explained that conference contract." Then *disillusionment*: "She doesn't like you. She'll probably resign Monday morning. And the rest of the office staff will resign, too—after they've set your desk on fire."

I was embarrassed to admit that I'd spent twenty-four hours being grumpy (my discouragement coping mechanism) over such a tiny disappointment.

Having identified my disappointment, I knew what to do. On Monday morning, I went straight to my assistant and asked, "Are you unhappy with me? I noticed that you were frowning as I left the office Friday."

Surprised, she said, "I don't remember frowning. What are you talking about?"

Relieved, I went back to my desk sorry to have wasted a Saturday. But I learned something about myself—I have a propensity to read too much into people's body language and facial expressions. Perhaps I'm too concerned that I be well liked.

You probably have your own hot buttons for discouragement. And here is why it's a big deal: Discouraged believers are (for that time period) liabilities to the Kingdom. They cannot serve others, because they are preoccupied with personal pain. They don't ask how *others* are doing, because they are preoccupied with how *they* are doing. Discouraged believers are takers—not givers.

In my daily-appointment-with-God journal, I have a line that says, "Any disappointments in the last twenty-four hours?" That question forces me to identify the breeding ground for discouragement and diminishes its power before it starts.

Does knowing the Four Ds bring courage to the discouraged? Not always. It's only a first step. The pain of a huge disappointment—such as a job loss, a wayward child, or an unexpected death in the family—will not go away just because you understand the process. But I have found great help in asking these four difficult questions:

1. What is my disappointment—specifically?
2. What self-doubts are going through my mind?
3. Are subjective speculations racing through my mind?
4. What coping mechanisms am I using to combat the discouragement?

Though the writer of Psalm 42:5 was deeply discouraged, he finished with: "Hope in God, for I shall again praise Him, the help of my countenance, and my God" (verse 11).

The psalmist was right to ask "Why are you in despair, O my soul?" But knowing why does not end discouragement. Now it is time to go back to the old hymn and "take it to the Lord in prayer" to receive the "help of His presence."

fear is only for wimpy christians

I REMEMBER THE DAY I RELUCTANTLY admitted I had fears. I was sitting at our kitchen table in Iowa City doing a Bible study on fear—not sure why I was even using precious time to do such a basic study. I'd been a Christian for many years, and in addition to my job at a newspaper, I was leading a ministry of evangelism and discipleship.

I thought only weak Christians had fears—certainly not leaders! Fear was surrendered at the cross. But "just in case," I began looking up verses on fear because I'd experienced some disconcerting behaviors the past year. For example:

- I found myself avoiding a dedicated leader in our ministry. He was bold, opinionated, and popular, but I was having mental arguments with him.
- After we set up our registration booth to meet freshmen students, I looked for excuses not to go in.
- I was spending an inordinate amount of time on my hobby—collecting tropical fish. I spent hours in front of my ten-gallon aquarium eating chocolate ice cream and staring at guppies, platys, and black mollies. I daydreamed about a bigger aquarium.

- I worried what people thought of me. Wanting to succeed so badly, I said and did what I thought important people in my world expected.
- I felt tired—even after a good night's sleep.
- Normally affable and gregarious, now I wanted to be left alone.
- I daydreamed about taking a vacation, if not for two weeks then maybe a few days, or a few hours or maybe even just to go to a movie late in the afternoon.

I didn't tell anybody about any of this stuff, but I knew something was wrong. I thought maybe I was using my time poorly, so I attended seminars to learn how to be more efficient. I also tried to be more consistent in the spiritual disciplines, such as devotions, prayer, and Scripture memorization.

Bear in mind that I'm not talking about fear of heights or small spaces. Those are built-in God-given fears that can save our lives. Despite my increased efforts at spirituality, I soon found myself with a bowl of ice cream while staring at my fish. But finally I went to the kitchen table and began mechanically looking up verses on fear. One word from Psalm 56:3 changed my life: "When I am afraid, I will put my trust in Thee."

The word *when* stopped me. Not *if* I am afraid, but *when*. The psalmist had fears and admitted them to the Lord. Was he an immature believer when he wrote this? Not likely.

Immediately, I saw that the hours in front of my aquarium and my longing for time off were escapes to avoid dealing with fear. Worry, people-pleasing, and wanting to be alone were additional symptoms.

Within minutes of finding Psalm 56:3, I honestly admitted my fears to the Lord one by one. I named people I was afraid of, including the sharp leader in our ministry. I identified situations that scared me, like making cold sales calls and confronting the accounting department.

Finding the word *when* released the pressure valve of my tightly wound performance-oriented life.

Why is admitting our fears so powerful? Because there is great power in honesty and humility. To say "I am afraid" brings me into a trust relationship with God like a child who grabs his father's outstretched hand when an aggressive dog comes by. Admitting fear triggers a loving response from our heavenly Father. It doesn't make the fear go away any more than the dog goes away. It gives confidence you will not be mauled.

But it's not easy to admit our fears.

I once led a ministry team that had worked together for years and had enjoyed a great working relationship as good friends. But we'd never talked about our fears. So it seemed appropriate one morning near the end of a staff meeting to innocently ask, "What would you say are a couple of your personal fears—things that scare you now and then?"

No one answered. I volunteered a couple of my fears to get the discussion started. Still, there was silence. We all shifted in our seats. No one said anything. Finally, I closed the meeting in prayer.

A few days later, I asked each meeting participant privately as to why no one had spoken before. They said that though they felt safe to speak in the environment of grace we had created they confessed they had never publicly admitted fears.

The apostle Paul admitted his fears: "And I was with you in weakness and in fear and in much trembling" (1 Corinthians 2:3). Toward the end of his ministry, Paul received reassuring words from the Lord at Corinth, that great cosmopolitan city given over to the worship of idols. The Lord's words are recorded in Acts 18:9-10: "Do not be afraid any longer, but go on speaking and do not be silent; for I am with you."

Even with much ministry experience behind him, Paul needed to hear words of comfort related to his fear. So you're in good company. Both the psalmist and the apostle Paul admitted their fears.

Now, how do we overcome the fears we've humbly admitted?

When I fear a specific person, I try to pray for him or her. Then, when I am with that person, I feel less intimidated. Also, I move toward the person or situation I fear because avoiding fears makes them worse. Just this morning, though I dreaded it, I phoned an old friend who had written me a critical letter about a doctrinal issue. I think he expected a public relations type ho-hum response by mail, and even though I would have felt more comfortable writing a pacifying note, I chose to move closer to him with a phone call. Interestingly, I feel more confident since I took the initiative to phone, and he told me twice how much he appreciated the call, even though we disagreed on the issue. Avoidance solves nothing. Thus, I've adopted the acronym that guides me. It is MTYP: Move Toward Your Problems.

In confronting fear, sooner or later I come back to my life promises. In fearful situations, I try to remember that God has promised to bring fruit out of my life. John 15:16 is a promise that all believers can claim: "You did not choose Me, but I chose you, and appointed you, that you should go and bear fruit, and that your fruit should remain." That word *go* requires risk. Too often, that idea of *going* is applied to missionaries embarking on a journey to the other side of the world. But it also applies to phoning a disgruntled friend or inviting a nonbelieving neighbor to dinner. Going requires taking initiative even though it is scary. I am helped to tackle my fears when I understand that risking is part of walking with Christ. And that implies dealing with my fears. I say, "Lord, I'm scared of this, but here I go. I'm counting on you for fruit."

Okay, how about you? Is it time to list your specific fears? Jot them down in front of that fish tank and ice cream!

everyone worries sometimes — what's the big deal?

OFTEN ASK BELIEVERS, "IS WORRY a sin?"

They smile sheepishly and say, "Everybody worries."

Bible commentator William Barclay said, "There may be greater sins than worry, but very certainly there is no more disabling sin."[1]

In the book *Every Other Bed*, author Mike Gorman explains that half the hospital beds in America are occupied by patients brought there, directly or indirectly, because of worry.[2]

Worry nearly disabled me — the chief of secret worriers. As an energetic college graduate, I tackled my first job at a newspaper with gusto. In addition, I was a conscientious father of two young daughters. And we participated in a ministry at the local college campus, often hosting students at our modest duplex. Life was exciting!

I took my job and ministry to heart — to heart in a good way, but I was overly conscientious. I couldn't shut down my mind, even as I lay in bed. And if students (who came from wildly dysfunctional backgrounds) didn't show up for Bible study, I became deeply concerned. Soon I noticed a pain in my upper stomach, usually around bedtime. It persisted no matter what foods I ate. Alma suggested I see a doctor. An outlandish idea! Brave males throughout history have always believed that going to a doctor is for sissies. I lasted three more days.

I told the doctor that "nothing serious" was wrong—I just wanted a checkup.

"Nobody comes here for a checkup," he said bluntly. "What's wrong?"

Outsmarted, I confessed, "My stomach hurts, up here at the top. "

He diagnosed the beginning of a duodenal ulcer and prescribed relaxation. "Don't always be on duty, " he said. That was embarrassing because I considered myself too spiritually mature to have an ulcer. As a teenager, I had memorized Ralph Waldo Emerson's poem:

Many of your ills you have cured,
And the strongest you have yet survived;
But what torments of grief you endured,
From evils that never arrived.[3]

The scary part was that I didn't even recognize that I was worrying. Had I not made changes, I would have occupied one of those hospital beds Gorman wrote about. Since then, I've observed worry-management strategies employed by many people (some are the same as discouragement-avoidance ploys):

- Denial: To quote Alfred E. Neumann of *Mad* magazine, "What, me worry?"
- Escape: Oversleep, oversex, overeat, overwork.
- Mental arguments: Replay the circumstances over and over in the mind.
- Depression: Wish life could be different.
- Abdication: Ignore responsibilities—like the father in the TV show "Everybody Loves Raymond." When confronted with a difficulty, he blurts out, "Who cares?" And the audience laughs.

But these tactics solve nothing. Lots of our strategies mask worry but don't effectively deal with it. What about this one, which is popular among Christians: "I'm not *worried*—just *concerned*!"

Concern is good. Jesus said God is concerned about even a sparrow falling to the earth. Paul was concerned for all the churches. But concern leaps to worry when we take circumstances into our own hands rather than looking to God for His grace. Concern plus God's grace equals peace. Concern plus my coping mechanisms equals worry.

So is worry a sin? An overlooked phrase in Luke 21:34 gives insight:

Be on guard, that your hearts will not be weighted down with dissipation [unrestrained indulgence in pleasure] and drunkenness and the worries of life, and that day come on you suddenly like a trap.

In listing all three behaviors together, Jesus implies that worries are as serious as dissipation and drunkenness. A church member who indulges in dissipation and drunkenness will quickly draw the attention of his pastor, but is indulging in the "worries of life" any less sinful?

Furthermore, what about Matthew 6:25-34 where Jesus said three times, "Do not worry"? Surely, He means, "*Try not* to worry"?

Singer Bobby McFerrin told us in the 1980s, "Don't worry—be happy!" A catchy song for sure, but he gave us no rationale to avoid worry. By contrast, Jesus gives solid reasons. Do not worry because:

- Your heavenly Father cares for you (Matthew 6:25-26).
- Worry will not add a single cubit to your life (Matthew 6:27).
- Your heavenly Father knows what you need (Matthew 6:31-32).
- Tomorrow has enough trouble of its own (Matthew 6:34).

Two of these reasons make common sense: worrying about tomorrow does no good (verse 34), and worrying does not "add a cubit to [our] life" (verse 27).

But the "heavenly Father" comments go to the heart of the problem. If God cares for birds (verses 25-26) and if He knows what we truly need (verses 31-32), why would we worry? What is it about the Fatherhood of God we don't understand?

What is the real culprit behind worry? Fear. Fear that I will not be provided for. Worry is a symptom of giving in to the fear that lurks behind it. Worry is choosing to fear rather than to trust. And that's why it's a sin.

Let me offer some practical suggestions that have helped me — starting way back with my duodenal ulcer diagnosis:

1. Quickly identify when you are tempted to worry. The temptation is not the sin. Bring it to God immediately.
2. Say thank you often. Philippians 4:6-7 is the classic verse on worrying: "Be anxious for nothing, but in everything by prayer and supplication *with thanksgiving* let your requests be made known to God. And the peace of God, which surpasses all comprehension, shall guard your hearts and your minds in Christ Jesus." Saying "thank you" by faith brings peace.
3. Limit mental arguments. Unlimited mental arguing ("he said, she said"), replaying the circumstances over and over, only makes me more agitated. Now I allow myself two mental reviews to learn a lesson or find an action to take. It's too bad most of us stop at Philippians 4:7. Verse eight says to "let your mind dwell on these things." What things? Things that are "true, honorable, and right." Mental arguments are usually not true, honorable, and right but merely speculation.
4. Realize that most "what-ifs" never come to pass. Just because your daughter is dating a 280-pound tattooed

California biker boy doesn't mean you should worry about what to serve his divorced hippie parents at Thanksgiving. Or if your husband is twenty minutes late coming home from the office, calling the emergency room is premature. Emerson's line "from evils that never arrived" was right.

We believers are being duped. We have the symptoms of worry but do not call it what it is: wrong choices before a heavenly Father who promises to provide. Unlike Jesus, Christians often do not consider worry a sin — it's certainly not one of the evangelical biggies. But it is just as disastrous. How many hospital beds today are filled with believers who need not be there?

harboring a little resentment can't hurt

I THOUGHT I KNEW MYSELF PRETTY well. But I made a surprising discovery starting at 10:00 a.m. on a Tuesday morning in Minneapolis.

I was at the office shouting into the phone to a pointy-headed conference-center director who couldn't get our key men's event onto his calendar. I slammed down the phone.

An hour later I was still angry—not only at the conference director, but also at the unfinished projects lying on my desk. Then it occurred to me that I had been angry all week. All month. All year.

Now the self-talk began: *I rarely explode like this. People compliment me on my easygoing nature. Maybe I'm working too many hours.*

What was lurking below the surface that brought on the angry explosion? The word *resentment* came to mind, a slow burning bitterness. Uh-oh! Was this affable Iowa farm kid becoming a resentful, bitter 40-year-old? Isn't bitterness for old people? I felt like I had discovered carbon monoxide in my soul.

Though it was only 11:00 a.m.—a little early for a lunch break—I grabbed my Bible and a notepad and determined to see what the Lord might say to me about resentment. He and I met at a fine dining establishment next door—Godfather's Pizza. I sequestered myself in a corner booth and ordered a small sausage pizza and a Diet Coke the size of a kitchen wastebasket. Not knowing where to begin, I checked the concordance at the back of my Bible for the word *grudge*. I wasn't prepared for what I found.

Esau "bore a grudge" against his brother Jacob (Genesis 27:41). Why? You might know the story. Esau, the elder son, was to receive the family inheritance from Isaac, his aged father, who was blind and ready to die. Isaac sent Esau out to hunt for wild game to prepare for the celebration. In the meantime, Jacob, the younger son, and his mother, Rebekah, plotted to deceive blind old Isaac into giving the blessing to Jacob. When Esau came back from hunting, he was told that his brother had stolen the family inheritance. Esau determined to get revenge by killing Jacob.

Then angry Esau did one more curious thing. He knew that his father and mother did not want him to marry a Canaanite woman, but that is exactly what he did.

Sitting at Godfather's Pizza, I discovered two ways a smoldering grudge revealed itself: *revenge* and *rebellion*. Hmm.

Then I turned to the book of Judges and studied Naomi, who after losing her husband and two sons, changed her name to "Mara," which means "bitterness."

As my lunchtime lengthened, I discovered that Bible characters who experienced crushing disappointments were top candidates for resentment. Disappointment, big or small, is the starting point of resentment. And who is without disappointment? For example:

- Job lost his fortune, then his family.
- Hannah could not have a child.
- Joseph was sold into slavery by his brothers.
- Samson lost his wife.
- Tamar was raped.

Next I saw that with each disappointment came dashed dreams or unfulfilled expectations. Esau would not become powerful and wealthy.

That honor would go to Jacob. Naomi would never have grandchildren. And so on. Disappointment has painful implications.

Third, I noted that resentment always had a target. Esau was angry toward his brother, and probably also his mother and blind old Isaac.

Naomi was likely resentful toward her husband for taking the family down to Moab in the first place and then dying, leaving her alone with no means of provision in a foreign land.

It has been said that all bitterness ultimately targets God. It is likely that Esau also blamed God for "allowing" him to be cheated. Naomi might have blamed God for causing the famine that prompted her family to move to Moab.

I left the pizza joint that day deeply humbled. I had discovered why I shouted into the phone and realized that I, too, was a candidate for resentment.

I continued to study Esau, Naomi, Joseph, and others over the next couple months, but my meditations took an unexpected twist. When I tried to identify the targets of *my* resentment, I couldn't find anyone or anything. Mom and dad? No, I had a good home.

I could find no target.

Then I realized the target was *me*. I was mad at myself for my own bad decisions. I had no one to blame but myself, and I did it daily by having unrealistically high standards, by driving myself toward workaholism, not being able to accept a compliment, and occasionally shouting into the phone. But I didn't know what to do about it.

Six months after the Bible study at Godfather's, traveling from Denver to Minneapolis, a snowstorm diverted our flight to Chicago. The airline put the passengers up overnight at a low-budget motel. Since it was also snowing in Chicago, I had nowhere to go even to eat. So I took it as a signal from the Lord to deal with the one toward whom I felt the most resentment — me.

I sat at the Formica-topped round table in the motel room and pretended that the person who had hurt me most — Scott — was sitting

across the table from me. I told him I forgave him for all his bad judgment and lousy decisions. I felt a little like Jimmy Stewart with his
imaginary six-foot rabbit in the movie *Harvey*.

After I told "Scott" how he had hurt me, I said a prayer similar to
this:

> Lord, I am in danger of becoming a resentful person. My symp-
> toms are discouragement, moodiness, and sometimes shouting
> into the phone. I do not feel others have hurt me, but I am
> hurting myself with my overly conscientious criticisms and
> overly high expectations and a subtle dislike of myself.
>
> I now choose to forgive Scott for past sins. I refuse to be
> harder on Scott than you are, heavenly Father. I now gladly
> give to Scott the same grace that Scott extends to others when
> they sin against him. Amen.

Why am I telling you this? Because many well-meaning people
are not aware of the slow burning resentment in their lives. They have
learned to stifle angry explosions, but they smolder inside even as they
pretend everything is fine. Following my lunch at Godfather's I asked
myself the following questions:

- What are *my* disappointments?
- What are *my* dashed dreams?
- Who is the target of *my* resentment?
- How does *my* resentment display itself?

Is it time for you to ask yourself these questions? Don't wait until
you're shouting into the phone. Maybe you and the Lord need to have
lunch together!

your self-esteem is determined by others

WHEN I WAS IN THE SEVENTH grade, my junior-high basketball coach called me "sparrow legs." I was at the drinking fountain when it happened. Everybody laughed. I laughed, too, but only to keep from crying.

Actually, I did have sparrow legs. They looked like Tinker Toy sticks coming out of my gym shorts. Although I never heard anyone call me that again, whenever I saw people in the gym whispering, I just knew they were talking about me. I hid in the back row for team pictures.

From seventh grade until my senior year in high school, I played in nearly a hundred basketball games. In every game I pulled my purple and gold trunks down as far as possible, and I yanked my socks up so only two inches of sparrow leg would show.

In my senior year for the team picture, we first stringers stood in the front row with our hands clasped behind our backs and our legs slightly spread like we were tough guys. I dreaded what the team picture would reveal. When the photos came back, to my surprise, my legs looked pretty much like everybody else's—same length and width and shape. They didn't look like sparrow legs at all. I'd grown and didn't even know it.

What a shock! Yanking up my socks had been unnecessary. As was the secret cursing I did of the coach who gave me the nickname. And all those sleepless high school nights wondering if I was attractive to girls!

For five years, I chose to cling to a two-word jest from a person important to me. My self-confidence was controlled for five years by an offhanded humorous remark. I gave another person the power to control me for five years.

Like me, nearly everyone is haunted by memories of unkind words spoken by a person important to them. Perhaps you've heard about the kid who thought his name was "Dammit Bob," because that's all he heard from his parents. Here are other hard-to-forget comments made to friends of mine:

- Bruce's father was introducing his children to a local dignitary. As the dad pronounced each child's name, he added a brief commentary. When he came to Bruce, he said, "And this is Bruce, the dumb one."
- Cindy's father told her, "You were a mistake. We never intended to have you."
- A new believer in Christ was told by a senior mentor, "You'll never make it."
- A young executive was told by his boss that he "just wasn't leadership material."

Unchecked, the harsh words of others can control us. Unless we deal with them, they dictate our self-worth, our confidence, and our happiness. Furthermore, the more important we consider the critic, the deeper the words cut. If a stranger had teased me about my sparrow legs, it wouldn't have hit me so hard. But coming from my coach, that hurt.

Years later, during a Big Twelve baseball game at Iowa State, I was standing next to the backstop waiting my turn to bat when a smart-aleck kid from the stands hollered, "Hey, lefty! Ride a horse much?" He was referring to my bowed legs. Great! Now I have *bowed* sparrow legs.

But I just turned and smiled. "Not much," I said. I never thought about it again. If a coach had made that comment, I would have dwelt on it for weeks.

How about you? Do words from your past haunt you?

Perhaps you've discovered how fruitless it is to argue mentally about the truth or untruth of "sparrow legs" statements (and maybe you heard much worse than that). Even if the person who labeled you was inaccurate or a jerk, the mind games sap your emotions. Also, replaying critical remarks in your head promotes bitterness—even if you choose not to believe the unkind comments.

I have concluded the only way to overcome hurtful labels is to establish a new identity based on who Christ says we are. For example:

- I am God's workmanship. "For we are His workmanship" (Ephesians 2:10).
- I am not condemned. "No condemnation for those who are in Christ Jesus" (Romans 8:1).
- I am "owned" by God. "You are a chosen race, a royal priesthood, a holy nation, a people for God's own possession" (1 Peter 2:9).
- I am valued, like a shepherd values his sheep. "The Lord is my shepherd" (Psalm 23).
- I am complete. "In Him you have been made complete" (Colossians 2:10).

Meditating on these phrases during the day or as I fall asleep at night helps me know my real identity, and the same will happen for you. Choose to replace the opinions of others with God's opinions. Proper self-worth means thinking about ourselves the way God thinks about us!

I can't change what people have said about me or might say in the future. But I can choose to think about myself from God's point of view—not my gym teacher's. When I say, "Don't focus on words from the past," I mean let them go *completely*. Hold on to them not even for one second. Stop those mental arguments. As soon as they come up, quit!

We all have a decision to make. We *decide* whose opinions will guide us. Consider this memo from a Hollywood agent rejecting an aspiring young actor: "Can't act. Can't sing. Can dance a little." What if Fred Astaire had chosen to dwell on these words? A newspaper fired a young reporter for not having good ideas! What if Walt Disney had concluded he wasn't creative?

Astaire and Disney chose not to let words from their pasts control their futures. And we don't have to either. Maybe you can't dance, maybe you have sparrow legs, or maybe someone said you were never going to be a leader, but don't play those tapes in your mind! Instead, dwell on the phrase, "I am God's workmanship." His opinion of you can be trusted. He died so He could give you a new identity. Keep *His* words about you in mind, and replay them over and over.

misconceptions about your schedule

sure, you're busy — it's unavoidable

"AMERICA: THE LAND OF THE RUSHED," complains small-town journalist Peg Zaemisch.[1]

I rush, too. Recently, while stuck behind a driver poking along in the left lane, I thought, *Get over in the slow lane with your slowpoke friends! I'm tired of waiting on you!*

Then I glanced at my speedometer. The "slowpoke" was actually exceeding the sixty-five-mile-per-hour speed limit. Even breaking the law was too slow for me! Embarrassed, I backed off the gas pedal.

Why is America so rushed? Many reasons, but most of us have too much to do and not enough time to do it. When arranging dinner with a friend, do we not schedule ninety days ahead—and still have difficulty finding an open slot?

Actually, the problem is not merely being busy, but being overbusy. And believers are the "overbusiest" of all! Ask a believer, "How are you doing?" What does she say? "Busy." And also "Tired." The world's view of Christians—busy *and* tired!

No wonder we're tired. Look what's happened to the amount of sleep we typically get. In 1850, Americans slept 9.5 hours each night. By 1950, it was down to 8 hours. Currently, it is 7 and declining.[2]

I recently posed a question at a seminar: What causes Christians to be overbusy? Here are responses from middle-aged, successful believers:

- "American culture is too busy, and we're caught up in it."
- "We lack the ability—or courage—to say no."
- "We've got to keep up with our kids."

But when the discussion turned to *why* we are so busy, they admitted soberly:

- Busyness boosts our self-esteem. Endless activity demonstrates to others and ourselves that we are important—maybe even spiritually mature. It's a badge of honor! We're needed, and we're doing lots of significant things.
- Busyness euthanizes our insecurity. If we stay busy, we don't have time to think seriously about our inner lives.

I appreciated the honesty of those at the seminar. The faster we go, the less we consider scary questions, such as: "Am I more Christlike now than I was twelve months ago? Am I compromising my values? Am I truly striving to live according to God's standards? Am I fantasizing in my thought life?" Let's face it, busyness is not next to godliness!

Consider the toll our hurried society takes on kids. It is not uncommon for twelve-year-olds to be involved in Scouts, traveling-team hockey, piano lessons, football, and the youth group at church. Add to these activities two hours of homework each night with an exasperated parent urging them on.

Author Mimi Doe says parents push their children to "manage their schedules as if they were little CEOs." She says that a kid's busy schedule often comes from overachieving, micro-managing parents.[3]

One ten-year-old said to his mother, "Can't we just stay home tonight?"

Kids need unstructured time to do "unproductive," non-video-game stuff—like sitting in the yard watching a parade of ants. Or pondering birds hunting for worms. Or daydreaming as billowy clouds roll across the sky. As a child, I spent glorious hours behind our machine shed, leaning over a fence while studying my dad's cows. But today, we rob kids of their childhood as we hurriedly chauffeur them from activity to activity in the name of good parenting.

A few years ago, I made a decision about busyness that changed my life. It was prompted by a phone call during a busy morning from an older missionary friend named Adrian. He politely asked how I was doing.

"Too busy. Honking at my taillights," I said in an attempt at humor, glancing at overdue reports on my desk.

Silence. I waited. Adrian was breaking a rule. Usually, when believers say how busy they are, listeners respond by describing how busy *they* are. Busyness face-offs, I call them.

After more silence, Adrian finally spoke: "Got a verse for you," he said.

Oh, great, I thought. *A Bible verse to patch my shattered nerves.* I steeled myself for a homily on serenity I was sure would follow.

"Sure, go ahead," I said halfheartedly. "What's your verse about my being too busy?"

"First John 1:9," he replied in deadpan tone of voice.

Recognizing the passage immediately, I was shocked. It says, "If we confess our sins, He is faithful and righteous to forgive us our sins and to cleanse us from all unrighteousness."

Did Adrian actually think I was sinning? Didn't he know that we were behind schedule? That money would be lost? That other departments were waiting for reports? It's not a sin — it's a way of life from which there is no escape!

After I hung up the phone, I decided I would deliberately choose a less busy lifestyle. I confessed that super-busyness did not honor the One who created me with limits.

Obviously, there are seasons of overbusyness. Tax accountants sleep at the office during March and April. And moms with two-year-olds have some long days (and many sleepless nights). But those seasons should be short-lived, the exception rather than the rule.

Look at Jesus. Did He rush frantically from activity to activity? Can you imagine Jesus answering a cell phone while taking little children in His arms?

True, Jesus had many demands on His time. At one point, so many people were coming and going that He and the Twelve had no time to eat (see Mark 6:31). But Jesus wasn't overbusy. Once, He sent the multitude away and instructed the Twelve to "come apart and rest" (Mark 6:31). In John 7, we read that He did not allow his brothers to push him into traveling prematurely to Jerusalem. And he waited two days before going to save sickly Lazarus (John 11). Busy, yes. Overbusy, no.

Interestingly, the word *rest* is used more than three hundred times in the Bible.

I wish I could tell you I've never been overbusy since Adrian's phone call. I still slip back into honking at my taillights sometimes. But here are the lifestyle decisions I'm trying to stick with:

- I use my cell phone only for outgoing calls; incoming calls are by prearrangement only with a few people to whom I've given the number.
- I rarely accept early-morning breakfast meetings.
- I do not accept extra responsibilities on the spot. I ask for time to consider the request. A missionary friend says, "Not every piece of luggage that comes off the conveyor has your name on it."
- I limit my work to 50 hours a week in the office and 65 hours when I travel. These limits force me to be efficient.

These lifestyle decisions may not work for you; your God-given capacities are unique. But here is a question I want to leave with you: Will you consider that an overbusy, rushed lifestyle might be a sin against your Creator?

you need to be available 24/7

A COUPLE DECEMBERS AGO, ALMA AND I received our annual Christmas letter from Larry and June, who live in Silicon Valley. After reviewing family and job news, Larry described how they could be contacted. It took half a page. Here is what he included:

- Home address
- Larry's personal e-mail (which had recently changed)
- June's personal e-mail
- Larry's work e-mail
- June's work e-mail
- Home phone number
- Larry's cell phone number
- June's cell phone number
- Larry's pager number
- June's pager number
- Larry's personal fax and business fax number
- June's business fax number

But he wasn't finished.

Next we got his business address and phone number, as well as

June's business address and phone number. And finally, Larry gave his new website address: www.alwaysonduty.com.

We knew Larry was exaggerating—but not much! As I put his letter in the Christmas pile with other green and red hard-to-read-small-print letters, I smiled. How did we survive before we had the technology to allow us to rush through airports shouting, "Can you hear me now?"

We are never off duty. Bosses frantically phone from the car, from home, during lunch at Amanda's Mexican Eatery. I agree that cell phones can help us get more done—at least I *think* I agree. But have we gone too far?

It is common to see two people eating "together" at a restaurant with one talking on the phone and the other quietly picking at her food. Women talk on cell phones while trying on dresses at Dillard's. Moviegoers are reminded *not* to use their phones. During the World Series, we see fans sitting behind first base talking on their phones. During the World Series!

At a high school homecoming football game last Friday, I was surrounded by seventy-five high school students talking on their phones. And mostly they were saying, "Nothing, what are *you* doing?" They were probably talking to one another.

It gets worse. A young guy in a snazzy suit came out of a bathroom stall at O'Hare Airport talking excitedly into his phone, the flushing noise of the toilet still providing "background music." He hurried past a line of guys standing at urinals talking on *their* phones. I'm not making this up.

Of course, cell phone dependency is just one way to add frenzy to our lives. We no longer stop working at 5:00 or 6:00 or 7:00 p.m., because a lot can be done in the car on the way home. Once home, we hurry to the computer to check e-mail or to see if the kids left messages as to their whereabouts. While on the computer, we get an instant message from someone who wants an instant answer to a question that could surely wait until tomorrow. Next, we check our home phone for voice messages. In the meantime, we have three missed messages on our cell phone.

Fashion dictates that we wear our cell phones on our hips like Old

West gunslingers. How about a quick draw contest?

Enough. What is going on here? Is technology the issue? No. Somehow, somewhere, with the aid of technology, a subtle decision has been made:

We must be available to the world 24/7.

We may not have realized we made this decision—or maybe it was made for us. Are we all 24/7 victims, unable to stop the rush to the technology sea? At least we can contact one another as we plunge over the cliff.

The need to be constantly in touch may have several causes:

- Insecurity. Do we fear being alone with our thoughts? What if we discover we are not happy?
- Exalted sense of our importance.
- Workaholism. Technology gives workaholics the ability to more easily tie up others with their projects. Cool.
- Boredom. Instead of eating when we're bored, we phone!

Did God create us to be available 24/7? Or did He make us with limits—like needing six to eight hours of sleep each night? Even Jesus ensured some "down time" in the midst of a busy schedule. Look at Luke 5:16: "But He Himself would often slip away to the wilderness and pray."

Notice the word *often*. Jesus habitually slipped away from people to be alone with the Father. His Bible study group did not accompany Him!

Also, He went to the *wilderness*—out into the solitude of nature. He did not go to daydream but to pray to the Father. If peace and quiet were essential for the sinless Son of God, what about us? Today, if we go to the wilderness, we take our phones.

As I mentioned in the last chapter, I no longer take incoming calls on my cell phone unless they are prearranged. I am not reacting to technology—I am not opposed to technology per se. What I'm reacting to is the subtle philosophy that says I must be available 24/7.

Though I want my credit card company and my doctor to be available around the clock, I have made the politically incorrect decision that I will *not* be on duty all the time.

I tell you this so you will think twice about your attachment to your cell phone, computer, or any other device that keeps you tethered to an invisible leash. Will the world come to an end if you are out of touch for a few hours (or even a few days)? If your kids can't reach you at the restaurant as you spend a quiet evening with your spouse, will it sear their self-esteem? Will your church's ministry come to a screeching halt if you can't be immediately contacted about a committee meeting or an upcoming service project?

A society that cannot be alone is a society that develops shallow people. Being alone with our thoughts might be scary, but it has the potential to produce depth as we ponder God, the universe, why we do what we do, why ants travel single file, and what happened in the 70s that made grown men wear platform shoes! Solitude can provide answers!

The decision to be available 24/7 is the problem, not technology. Technology simply exposes our insecurities.

Am I advocating giving your cell phone or other communication gadgets to Goodwill? Certainly not! But try this: Just for a day, disconnect, power off, shut down the electronics. Just for a day. Learn to appreciate the discipline of solitude.

God didn't create you to be on duty all the time. That's His job. He's available every second of every day—and therefore, you don't have to be. George Herbert, in his poem "Be Alone," captured it well:

> By all means use some time to be alone,
> Salute thyself; see what thy soul doth wear,
> Dare to look in thy chest; for 'tis thine own;
> And tumble up and down what thou find'st there.[1]

Be alone! Don't be on duty 24/7. I dare you.

misconceptions about relationships

CHAPTER 22

you can't help but be a little judgmental

I HAVE A CONFESSION: SOME CHRISTIANS embarrass me. Not all of them, just those who in my opinion don't represent the cause of Christ well. For example, whenever TV networks interview evangelicals, they somehow discover interviewees who seem out of touch, narrow-minded, or speak in Christian clichés.

I want Christians to be articulate on national television with hopes that the gospel is advanced. But I shudder when Christians speak in public. Perhaps I'm too judgmental. But, honestly, aren't you sometimes embarrassed by your fellow believers?

Another confession: I'm embarrassed by non-public believers, too—like the big-haired Christian woman who showed up at our neighborhood garage sale. I gave her a cheerful "Good morning" as she meandered up to browse through clothes our children had outgrown, Christmas gifts from the 90s we didn't have the courage to "regift," and some Christian books I'd laid out so I could fill my shelves with more. The woman was attractive and tall, perhaps 5'7" but appearing to be 6'2" with her hair piled high. She wore tight orange capri pants, and her lips were painted deep red. Tanned and outfitted with stylish sunglasses, she had long, orange fingernails that gave her hands a claw-like appearance reminiscent of those animals that dig for ants on the

Nature Channel. She turned the head of everyone in the driveway.

Then it happened.

Holding up a Christian book and over the noisy chatter of other shoppers, she called to me in a booming voice, "Are you a Christian?" Every conversation in the driveway stopped. Every head jerked around to find me, twenty feet away, busy with another customer. Silence.

Two dozen pairs of eyes riveted on me as everyone awaited my answer. *Am I a Christian?* I thought. I knew I was, of course, but I found myself reluctant to verbalize my faith commitment. My mind raced. If I said yes, my customers might roll their eyes and think that I was "tacky" like her. If I said no, I would deny the most important Person in my life. Why was that so hard?

Instead of shouting across the driveway, I calmly walked over to her. Quietly, I said, "Yes, I am a Christian." But I didn't feel like a very good one. "Are you a Christian, too?" I meekly inquired.

"Yes," she said. "My husband and I are starting a church south of town."

"Great!" I responded, wondering if she wore her badger claws on hospital visits. "Hope it goes well."

Then she drifted off to peruse other merchandise. I stood quietly for a moment, wondering why I didn't like her. Why wasn't I elated that a new church was starting? Why was I so unaccepting?

I thought I learned to "accept others" years ago through a difficult God encounter at the newspaper where I worked. I went out to lunch with Gary, a fellow advertising rep and a dedicated believer. Though not verbal about his faith, everyone respected him, even though he periodically lost his temper with the accounting department. Who didn't?

Gary turned out to be a good listener, so over our sandwiches, I felt free to criticize a couple churches in our community. Gary listened politely. He asked a question or two to challenge my thinking, but I was strong in my opinions. Back at the office, as I let him out of the car, his anger popped out.

"Scott," he said, trying to keep his voice from cracking, "you are way too judgmental." Then he blurted like a machine gun, "Just because these Christians are different from you, they are still your brothers and sisters in Christ, and you are going to spend eternity with them in heaven so you better get used to the idea of loving people who don't hold the same opinions as you. In fact, Scott, you need them. They have much to contribute to you. Thanks for lunch."

And he slammed the door.

I was stunned. Then angry. Then hurt. But as I parked the car, I waded past his anger to his words. He was right. I was unaccepting. Who was I to condemn my fellow believers with whom I will spend eternity? Why did I feel compelled to criticize people who thought and lived a little differently than I did?

Shortly after Gary's scolding, I discovered Romans 15:7: "Wherefore, accept one another, just as Christ also accepted us to the glory of God."

Christ has accepted me with all my foibles; therefore, I must accept others. When I fail to accept others while still expecting Christ to accept me, that's hypocrisy. How dare I reject others whom Christ has accepted, including loud, big-haired ladies.

I thought I had learned that lesson years ago, but here I am at the garage sale with a critical spirit.

At the risk of sounding judgmental, I think all of us are too judgmental. One of the watching world's biggest criticisms of Christians is that we are too disapproving and condemning. A worldly wise seatmate on an airplane confided in me, "Christians are so judgmental. I'm definitely not into judgment."

The Bible has much to say about people with a judgmental attitude. Two seemingly contradicting gospel passages grab my attention. The most well known is Matthew 7:1, where Jesus said, "Do not judge lest you be judged." The context says we are not to "pass sentence" on a brother with a speck in his eye while we have a "log" in ours. Fair enough. I should not pass sentence on the big-haired lady. But Jesus also said, "Do not judge according to appearance, but judge with righteous judgment" (John 7:24).

Okay, which is it? Did Jesus say it is okay to judge so long as we do it righteously?

The Greek word for judge—*krino*—has several applications. In Matthew, it implies "assuming the office" of a judge or "passing sentence," but in John it implies simply to "form an opinion."[1]

The problem with most of our "judging" is that we pronounce a sentence rather than formulate a discerning opinion. I'm not trying to let you (and me) off the hook here, but we must distinguish between the two meanings. "Judge not" implies that we accept and love our fellow Christians, but it does not imply we are to foolishly go along with every goofy thing they do.

I realize now that what bothered me most wasn't the garage-sale woman's gaudy appearance; it was her insensitivity of calling out in public, "Are you a Christian?" My opinion was that I thought the cause of Christ would be harmed by this method of spreading the faith. I think that's a discerning opinion, not a sentencing.

Though I accept my fellow believers, I need not pretend they are wise when they are not. Nor need I endorse their choice of hairstyle or method of witnessing. I don't need to sacrifice my insights just to "accept" a fellow believer. But I dare not pass sentence!

One other thing: It's not my job to judge what embarrasses our sovereign God. Maybe my judgmental attitude embarrasses Him more.

if it blesses you, it will bless others

JESUS SAID SEVEN WORDS THAT PUZZLE me. I've never heard a preacher—even a TV preacher—explain them. I've never seen a magazine article explain them. Friends recognize the passage but offer only rambling explanations.

These words are important because they're located near the end of Jesus' famous Sermon on the Mount. You've heard these seven words before. But before I reveal them, consider this related story from a friend I'll call Steve:

I had just gotten out of the hospital from ankle surgery. Doctor's orders were to stay on crutches for six weeks to avoid putting pressure on the screws in my left ankle. But I was also encouraged to practice using my crutches. My first outing was to "walk" a few doors down the sidewalk to pick up some mail delivered to the wrong house. I easily hobbled to Nancy's house even though my ankle throbbed.

Nancy handed me the mail, and I paused politely. Nancy had a good heart. She asked if I was in pain. That was nice.

"Yes, a little," I said, not wanting to compare pain stories with a woman who had experienced childbirth five times. Then she launched into the virtues of a calcium remedy for which she was the local distributor.

"It's a long-term solution, not a quick fix," she reminded me, then hurriedly excused herself to fetch a brochure. She was more excited than a Minnesotan at a potluck.

I shifted uncomfortably on my crutches.

Finally, she returned. I took the brochure and started to tuck it into my pocket. But she motioned for me to open it. She urged me to order these pills directly from her to save money. Her words burst forth like buttery movie popcorn. Ratt-tatt-tatt. Ratt-tatt-tatt.

She segued excitedly to her personal testimony of how these pills had so marvelously helped her — but I could stand no more. Smiling as best I could, I held up my right hand as if to say, "Stop!" I said I was sorry, but I needed to go home. My ankle hurt.

She immediately apologized and helped me out the door adding, "Let me know if you want those pills. It's all in the brochure."

Back to Jesus' seven words: "Do not throw your pearls before swine" (Matthew 7:6). Bible scholars say the early church used this verse to exclude from membership those who hostilely rejected the gospel. Don't throw the precious gospel before closed-minded, unteachable "swine."

But that doesn't fit with the Beatitudes two chapters earlier where Jesus says the Kingdom of God is open to anybody no matter what their spiritual condition (Matthew 5:1-12). This passage made no sense to me until I studied Dallas Willard's section on Matthew 5-7 in *The Divine Conspiracy* and reflected on my personal encounters with swine.

Back on the farm, it was my daily duty at 5:00 p.m. to carry four heavy five-gallon buckets of shelled corn to the concrete feeding floor where twenty-five hungry gestating sows awaited. At 4:45 p.m., the sows congregated, squealing and pushing at the worn wooden gate with their cute little pink piggy noses. (Actually, sows have huge, ugly vacuum-cleaner noses the size of Frisbees—but I digress.) For fifteen minutes, the sows milled around the feeding floor nuzzling the worn concrete, vacuuming for leftovers and squealing for "corn-boy." That was me.

To avoid getting knocked down by these ill-mannered pregnant females, I'd throw a few handfuls of corn to one side, and when they rushed after it, I quickly climbed into the feedlot and poured out their corn. Once eating, their squealing stopped.

Suppose instead of corn I had poured out a nice fresh bucket of yummy pearls. How would the hogs have reacted? They might have crunched them for a second or two, but soon they'd have spit them out and run their muzzle over the pearl pile looking for something of value. Annoyed, they would begin squealing again and move menacingly toward "pearl-boy" standing at the gate.

Suppose I had tried to reason with them: "My dear gestating lady swine, do not disdain the precious pearls I have laid before you. I paid dearly for them. They are more valuable than corn. Eat and enjoy." But pigs cannot appreciate pearls.

Back to Steve's story about the sales pitch from his neighbor. Nancy took something precious to her and sincerely tossed it to Steve (think of him as the "swine"). Though he wanted to draw nourishment from her medical "pearls," he could not appreciate them at that moment. He was in pain.

But I, too, am guilty. I regret the times I have overzealously pushed my agenda—whether it be sharing the gospel to a sleepy seatmate on an airplane, offering "fix-it" solutions to my family, or giving my opinion when it was not asked for.

Pushing pearls is sometimes simply bad timing, such as in Nancy's case, but sometimes it smacks of manipulation. Jesus saw it as a power play to move what is precious to us onto the backs of others who have no context for it. *We* feel better after we have pushed our pearls, but

Jesus said not to do it.

Furthermore, Jesus said the hogs "turn and tear you to pieces." If you've ever been the recipient of someone's pearl-pushing, you know how annoyed you feel. Pushing pearls creates animosity.

It's unfortunate that as we read this passage, we don't connect verses 7-11 to verse 6. Even in my Bible, there is a paragraph break and a subhead (added by an editor at some point). But these verses should be connected.

In verse 7, Jesus exhorts, "Ask and it shall be given you." Instead of *pushing* your precious pearls onto others, *ask* others to help you. They can say no, but asking puts the "askee" in the power position. If Nancy had asked, "Steve, when you feel better, could I tell you about this calcium medication?" He still might have said no, but he wouldn't have been annoyed. Asking brings people together. Pushing an agenda forces them apart.

The next time you are tempted to manipulate a conversation to make your point or get your way, humbly appeal to your conversation partner for help. Of course, this propels us back to trusting God because when we ask others for help we are asking Him also. Trusting— not pushing!

So now you know what has mystified Bible scholars for centuries. If only they had spent more time around impatient gestating swine!

leadership is primarily talking

A WELL-KNOWN CHRISTIAN COUNSELOR WAS the main speaker at a tiny conference center in the north woods of Wisconsin. Because it was a small event for young leaders, we were encouraged to meet the speaker personally. Many of us hoped to receive personal advice on walking with Christ, being good husbands, or balancing ministry responsibilities with full-time jobs.

My opportunity came right away—before the conference started. The famous speaker and I were assigned the same six-bed knotty-pine dorm room. The conference host introduced us and then left. Unpacking our suitcases took about fourteen seconds, and soon we were talking casually while sitting opposite one another on bunk beds. He asked how I'd become a believer. I answered nervously—and briefly. Then he asked about my life with Christ. I answered again, this time not so briefly.

Then he was silent. I wasn't used to that. I expected him to jump in with something from his own experience or a Scripture verse, but he didn't. So I continued to talk unhurriedly. He just listened. He didn't interrupt with a verse or an exhortation. I felt uneasy. What about the dead air hanging between us? I kept going. I didn't realize I had so much to say. Having time to compose my thoughts helped me understand what I actually believed.

For twenty minutes, this went on with him sitting on the top bunk leaning forward. Other guys were going in and out of the large bunk-room, but he ignored them. He seemed interested only in me. It felt strange, but I loved it. He gave me his most precious possession — personal attentiveness.

My bunkmate was doing something believers today (and especially leaders) find difficult — he listened without interrupting. He asked questions instead of giving answers. I found it engaging and appealing. But more than that, this man influenced me for life in that twenty-minute encounter. Today, people tell me I am a good listener and that I ask good questions rather than giving a steady stream of exhortations.

While I appreciate their feedback, I have not always followed the example of my conference bunkmate. For many years, I "hijacked" conversations — that is, I'd keep quiet until the other person said something that spurred an experience *I* wanted to tell about. Then I'd hijack his or her thought and explain my own. I thought I could lead people primarily by talking, exhorting, preaching, admonishing.

Furthermore, just because I stopped talking didn't mean I was genuinely listening. I was preparing what I would say next. Perhaps some of my exhortations were appropriate, but if I could do it over, I would talk less and listen more.

As the old joke goes, "I've talked about me long enough . . . now it's your turn to talk about me." But merely turning off the "me topic" is not the point. The point is to stop talking — period.

What is it about listening that has such power? Listening is powerful because it honors the person being listened to. It makes the speaker feel he or she is of value — even if they are talking nonsense. Psychiatrist Paul Tournier said, "It is impossible to overestimate the power of listening well and taking people seriously." Listening wins loyalty.

A listener is actually a servant. "Mighty mouths" inadvertently force others to serve them. By contrast, good listeners are not as interested in getting their own needs met as in meeting the needs of others. That is what happened in Wisconsin. I was served. And I was greatly influenced for the rest of my life.

Does this imply that a listener has no agenda? Certainly not! A listener can have an agenda—in fact, we all have agendas. That's okay. The problem is hiding our agendas and pushing our agendas too aggressively.

For example, a pastor wants to influence a young couple to start a small group Bible study. He has an agenda. He eloquently extols the importance of small groups and explains why it is good for the couple and the church. But if he doesn't discover that they botched their last attempt to lead a small group, he has missed a grand opportunity to help them deal with failure and fear. He may win compliance for a time, but he will not successfully "lead." Leading without listening makes people feel used, not developed.

Naturally, the Bible has a lot to say on this subject. For instance, Proverbs 18:13 warns, "He who gives an answer before he hears, it is folly and shame to him." An Italian proverb says it another way: "From listening comes wisdom, and from speaking, repentance."[1] But Proverbs 20:5 goes even further in showing us how to lead by listening: "A plan in the heart of a man is like deep water, but a man of understanding draws it out."

I visualize my conversation partner as having a deep well of fresh, cool water. As an attentive listener, I have the opportunity to discover (and maybe help him or her discover) what is in that well. So I draw it out with meaningful questions.

A caution here: I have occasionally overdone it with questions. People feel pressured if you pepper them with one question after another like a woodpecker attacking a sapling. Feeling awkward, they will look for the nearest exit. Slow down. Pauses are okay. Be genuine. Volunteer a sentence or two about your own weaknesses. Your compassion will show—as will your lack of compassion. You can be more influential by listening than you can by talking. Give a friend the gift of your complete attentiveness.

always have an agenda

S PENDING MORE THAN TWO HOURS WITH another person without an agenda is awkward for me. I like a clear game plan. I usually start my day with an agenda—a goal, a takeaway. And people tell me they like the fact that I don't hide my agenda. What you see is what you get. People also tell me I get a lot done.

So why do I always have to *accomplish something?* My assistant says I'm a workaholic. She's probably right.

Thankfully, my son, Andrew, is not a workaholic. He enjoys just hanging out. He's laid-back and is not bound by an agenda—which drives me nuts sometimes. But Andrew is teaching me a better way.

For Andrew's twenty-sixth birthday, I arranged for us to see a Colorado Avalanche hockey game. I knew he liked hockey but never realized what a rabid fan he was. He was thrilled. Beforehand, he quizzed me on when we would leave for the arena, where we would eat on the way, where the seats were, and so on. An NHL game would be a first for both of us.

Besides enjoying the game together, I wanted to talk about serious stuff, too. Honestly, I was hoping Andrew would solicit a little fatherly advice. The hockey game provided the opportunity.

We departed early so we wouldn't get caught in traffic during the seventy-five-minute drive to Denver, and we enjoyed a leisurely meal at a nearby restaurant before the game. Thirty minutes before start time, we were seated in the thirty-ninth row high above the ice. Andrew was jumping out of his skin with anticipation!

During the pregame drills and warm-up, we marveled at how big the players were and how fast they skated. Their uniforms were more colorful than on TV. The music was loud; two Zambonis glided across the ice picking up teeth; and remote-control mini-blimps flashed advertisements. We couldn't get enough of it. Oh, yeah, and we also liked the hockey game.

The Avalanche played poorly and lost decisively. When the game was over, I started to get up, but Andrew wasn't moving. So I sat back down. We stayed motionless in the thirty-ninth row for ten minutes as the fans filed out. Finally, I shuffled in my chair thinking it was time to go, but Andrew pulled me back.

"Let's just sit, Dad," he said.

He was clearly enjoying the moment. So we sat.

At long last, we decided it was time to head home. On the way, the weather turned snowy so we crept along at twenty miles per hour. And we talked — not only about the game, but also about issues Andrew was facing in trying to start a new career. But it was mostly small talk. No conclusions, no decisions, and no advice from Dad.

Finally, as the snow cleared near home, there was a lull in the conversation. Despite having no agenda, in my fatherly attempt to bring closure to the evening, I asked Andrew what was the highlight of his birthday trip to see the Avalanche.

He didn't answer immediately. Silence is unusual for my normally talkative son. I expected he might say the opening drop of the puck or maybe the nice meal before the game. Then I thought maybe my question put pressure on him. Did have an agenda after all? Finally, he responded, "Dad, the highlight was just being with you."

Now it was my turn to be silent. Just to be with me! Wow! I felt like shouting Sally Field's famous line after winning an Oscar: "You like me! You really like me!"

I am discovering as I grow older how easily *task* can overrun *people*. Task slyly sneaks up on us, causing us to hurry over the people God has providentially placed in our lives. But must there be a measurable "takeaway" from every relationship? Sometimes an agenda gets in the way. Sometimes it's good just to hang out!

Even though Jesus had an agenda, a mission, He could also hang out. As Mark 3:14 tells us, "And He appointed twelve, that they might be *with Him*, and that He might send them out to preach" (emphasis added). Here we have both *people* (with Him) and *task* (send them out to preach). Jesus didn't hang out with the Twelve simply for the sake of hanging out. He had a mission.

But we often overlook the phrase "that they might be with Him." Jesus wasn't afraid of spending more than two hours with the Twelve. He built friendships. Giving people your time honors them—and you needn't always accomplish something.

Andrew taught me a lesson on that snowy night. Today, I go more slowly with people. I'm not as hurried at business meetings. Every breakfast appointment doesn't have to end with "action items." I don't mind it as much when others chase conversational rabbits. I don't need closure for everything. Just hanging out with people—what a concept!

And what was the highlight of my hockey evening in Denver? Just being with Andrew.

PART SEVEN

misconceptions about family expectations

good parents never resent their children

LOVE MY KIDS. WELL, OKAY, I love my kids 95 percent of the time. But sometimes it's hard to love unappreciative, sullen-faced thirteen-year-olds whose worldview extends no farther than the mall. As Joey Bishop, a comedian in the early days of television, once quipped, "We'd have gotten divorced sooner, but neither one of us wanted custody of the kids!"

Unlike Joey Bishop, today's got-to-be-perfect-parents beat themselves up over their periodic dislike for their own flesh and blood. But face it—sometimes you can't stand your kids! It's okay. It is time to blow the whistle on overspiritualized denial. It doesn't mean you are a bad mother or a deadbeat dad. You are not alone. I was somehow morbidly encouraged when a guilt-ridden parent told me her story:

> I was driving my nine-year-old daughter home from an elementary school event. I can't even remember what it was. She and I had not been quarrelling. Nor was there a crisis at home.
>
> I distinctly remember glancing at her as she sat contentedly on the passenger side of our Chevy staring out the window and thinking to myself, *I don't like you.*
>
> Immediately, I felt guilty for such a thought. Don't good

moms gush with love for their children? Where did this animosity come from? This was a wonderful child—she was not a problem at school nor at home. When she needed correction, a stern look from her father made the point; she caught on immediately.

Maybe it was her attitude. Sassiness perhaps. Whatever it was, for the first time I was honest enough to admit that I sometimes resented my own child. It was eerie.

Occasional feelings of dislike for our children are . . . well, normal. I am certainly not condoning any kind of harm toward children—physical, emotional, or even spiritual. Parents who abuse their children need serious professional attention. I am simply saying it is time to wage war on denial and to be realistic about expectations. There's no point in pretending your annoyance—perhaps even disdain—doesn't exist. Wearing an everything-is-fine mask will not make it go away. In fact, denial further impedes learning to love your kids in deeper ways.

Here's what helps me: Understanding that the *feeling* is not the *sin*.

Many Christians assume that spiritual maturity is measured by the absence of ugly thoughts or "inappropriate" emotions. Wrong. Spiritual maturity is measured by what we do with these thoughts or feelings once they enter our consciousness. As the adage goes: "You can't stop birds from flying over your head, but you don't have to give them permission to build a nest in your hair."

Let's say you've just experienced a fleeting moment of dislike for your oldest child—the one who got a tattoo last week without your permission. Not that you would have given permission anyway, but it's not a tattoo that can be easily hidden beneath a wedding dress (should a wedding day ever come). Instead of plunging into guilt over what an unloving parent you are, tell God your feelings about the tattoo girl. Say something like this: "Lord, right now I can't stand being in the presence of this kid you gave me! I'm wondering if there was a mix-up at the hospital. And if not, why did you give me this person to raise?"

Yes, you can be that honest with God. He knows your heart. Own your feelings — don't ignore them. Take them to the Lord.

Ask Him to help identify what bothers you and why. What exactly is it that bugs you about your child? Though it is difficult, try to get beyond her annoying behavior. Is it possible that you see in her a weakness that you see in yourself? Often the things we dislike in others are the very things we dislike in ourselves. Maybe this is more about you than about your child.

Or does your child's behavior represent an unhealthy direction — something you need to deal with? Is there a deeper issue than a tattoo (broken curfews or obnoxious friends or offensive music)? Pray and correct. Merely overlooking offenses will not increase your love.

Loving someone doesn't mean you never become resentful of them. Are you not annoyed sometimes by others you are expected to love deeply — parents, spouse, or siblings? The *temptation* to express your annoyance in ungodly ways (considering searching the Yellow Pages for gypsies needing children) is not the sin. This annoyance gives you an opportunity to learn to love in a deeper way.

I noticed in Titus 2:4 that Paul admonishes the older women to "encourage the young women to love their husbands, to love their children." Why would the older women in Titus' church need to spend their precious time helping younger women love both their husbands and *children*? Is it possible that even the godly Christian women of the early church in Crete struggled to love their own family members? Sometimes we need to be reminded to love our children.

You are in good company. But you won't learn to love your children more by denying your true feelings. But after you've admitted it, then what? Two words: pray and serve. I've found that praying for those whom I sometimes dislike draws my heart back toward them. And when I serve those who annoy me — even if I serve them from a *decision* to love rather than from a *feeling* of love — my heart is drawn toward them.

Besides, if the gypsies accepted your offer, you know you'd miss them.

falling out of love?
it's over

MAYBE YOU'VE HEARD THE 50s TUNE on the "Oldies" radio station, "It's So Easy to Fall in Love." But if you're married, sooner or later, you'll find it easy to "fall out of love."

On your wedding day, you believed that you would forever love the adorable, generous, charming, saintly person standing beside you. Laughing at your wedding reception, you never imagined having an angry thought toward such a sensitive human being. You may have even told a gathering of friends, family, and assorted other witnesses how God led you together and that it was His will for you to marry.

Then the honeymoon ended. The courtesy your husband displayed during courtship tapered off. The jokes your wife used to laugh at now evoke groans and rolled eyes. You can't remember the last time he gave you a genuine compliment. She used to welcome your sexual advances but now she's just "too tired."

It may take a few months or a few years, but as your dashed dreams multiply, you'll wonder: *Have I fallen out of love? Did I marry the wrong person?* And you'll ask these questions no matter how spiritually mature you are!

You might even find yourself agreeing with the English poet Percy Byshe Shelly, who wrote, "A system could not have been devised more studiously hostile to human happiness than marriage." (Of course, he was married to Mary Shelly, the author of *Frankenstein*.)

Howard Hendricks, esteemed professor at Dallas Seminary, frequently said it this way: "Marriage is like flies on a windowpane. Those on the outside want in, and those on the inside want out."

Many dedicated Christians experience these feelings. Too embarrassed to acknowledge their pain, they endure dissatisfying or distant marriages, hoping something will change. They do not know what to do other than an occasional weekend away to fan smoldering romantic embers. Or they try remodeling the house or taking dance lessons or buying a boat—anything! Some pour their remaining emotional energy into their children, making each partner feel even more neglected.

They have "fallen out of love."

May I offer a couple of suggestions from the vantage point of forty-plus years of marriage to Alma?

First, don't try to remake the other person into a trophy husband or trophy wife, and don't compare your spouse with others. Hinting or even blatantly suggesting that he work out at the gym more frequently will backfire. So will a comment like, "Maybe you should join that Bible study of Bob's. He treats his wife so nice." Instead, try this: "Accept one another, just as Christ also accepted us" (Romans 15:7).

Admit your pain. Be honest enough to pray something like: "Lord, today I do not feel love for my husband. I do not want him to look at me or touch me. I would have had a better marriage with nasal-voiced comedian, Woody Allen. I'm dying here! I want out! Help me!" Can you be that brutally honest with the Lord? Sure, He understands your deepest longings.

Second, you can learn to love again. I experienced this on a northern Wisconsin camping trip when our kids were young. Each summer, I would drag Alma, three kids, and our dog, Toby, into the wilds of the Wisconsin woods to "relax." We didn't rent a camper trailer; we were tent-campers like Daniel Boone. No showers, no motels, and no whining. Strangely enough, we loved it.

On one particular vacation, though, I was discouraged and grumpy. I had been going through a tough time in my life with Christ, and I was overly busy at work and had neglected investing in my marriage for months. The third day on the camping trip, I couldn't sleep, so I got up at dawn, stirred up the campfire, and sat dejectedly in front of the tent while my family snoozed peacefully inside. I'm sorry to say that I blamed Alma and the kids for my sadness. The dog wouldn't even look at me.

It's not my fault, I reasoned. *I'm miserable because of them.*

Too embarrassed to admit I didn't love my family the way I should, I daydreamed of how my life might have been different had I never married in the first place—which made me feel horrible for even thinking such a thought.

So went my private pity party in the pines. I felt trapped.

Then out of nowhere came a succession of thoughts: *Fix breakfast for the family! What? In the middle of my pity party? No way.*

But the thought persisted: *Fix breakfast for the family!* Serve the people who were the "cause" of my misery? I don't feel like it!

At last, reluctantly, I got the fire roaring and retrieved the sixteen-pound cast-iron frying pan. I mechanically peeled potatoes for raw fries, mixed up some eggs, and soon had bacon sizzling. I can't say I *wanted* to do this—I just did it.

Soon from inside the tent, I heard a surprised sleepy hobbit whisper, "Is Dad fixing breakfast?" Out they came, one by one. And we had breakfast together in the cool woods.

Here is what surprised me: Before breakfast was over, I found myself genuinely enjoying my family. I began to feel loving affection for them in a genuine way within twenty minutes *as I served them.*

Can you regain genuine feelings of affection? Yes, but you must start by doing something you will not "feel" like doing. Serve her. Serve him. Serve them.

The world says that great sex is the measure of true love. But

Galatians 5:13 says, "Through love serve one another." The test of your love for your spouse is not great sex (as good as that is) but great service—*whether you feel like it or not.*

Nine years into our marriage, Alma and I got new wedding bands because our marriage had become so different from the one anticipated on our wedding day. We were only eighteen and nineteen when we got married and brand-new believers in Christ. Based on statistics, we would have split long ago! But our marriage changed because Christ changed our lives little by little. I asked the jeweler to engrave on Alma's new wedding band a phrase from Genesis about Isaac marrying Rebekah: "She became his wife; and he loved her" (24:67).

Alma and I loved each other plenty the day we were married, but we had no idea what biblical married love was all about. I learned to love her the way she deserved to be loved *after* we were married—not before. Note the order in the verse: first marriage, then love.

You are not alone in your feelings of "falling out of love" or wishing you had not married or thinking you married the wrong person or fantasizing about greener pastures. Every married person has these temptations.

By now, you may consider your spouse to be unlovable—especially compared to someone else, real or imaginary. Stop! Proverbs 5 warns against the greener-grass syndrome, and it starts with controlling our thoughts. Verse 19 says we are to "be exhilarated always with her love" as opposed to finding exhilaration in the arms of another. That requires a decision. Decide to be exhilarated with your spouse's love and his or hers alone.

Even if divorce is not your intent, fantasizing destroys love. If you become miserable enough, you will entertain thoughts of divorce no matter what your theology. Pain trumps theology.

Whether you feel like it or not, *invest* in your spouse. *Serve* your spouse, even if it seems mechanical at first. Keep at it. But what if he or she doesn't return your love? Continue serving. Demanding a response is manipulation. Doesn't Jesus keep on loving us whether we respond or not?

Have you married the wrong person? No. Are you loving in the wrong way? That's more likely. You can regain genuine love from this day forward by serving first. Don't give up. Fix breakfast!

CHAPTER 28

great parenting guarantees great kids

WHY IS IT THAT SOME GODLY parents have children who go
astray? And why is it that some ungodly, absentee parents have
godly, productive kids? Think for a moment of someone you know
who is a great parent but has a wayward child. And don't you know
kids with horrible backgrounds who love God and lead successful lives?
Go figure.

Two years ago today, as I write this chapter, my friend Bob in the
Midwest checked his adult daughter into a rehab center for drugs. It
broke his heart. Where did Bob and his wife, Stacy, go wrong in their
parenting? Or did they go wrong? Here's what Bob says:

I was thirty-one when our daughter [I'll call her Jesse] was born.
My best memories with her are playing "horsey" and wrestling
on the floor of our living room. And laughing. Lots of laughing. Her common refrain was, "Do it again, Dad!" She was a
happy kid.

As she got older, she and her sisters loved to play hide and
seek all over the house with Stacy and me on Saturday evenings.
They'd shout in delight when I emerged from my hiding place
and chased them back to base. I can still see her throwing her

head back gleefully as she ran.

During sixth grade, her gleeful spirit began to disappear. It saddens me even now to think of it. And I become tearful thinking of the pain she is in today as she packs her suitcase to go to rehab.

As for faith, she "received Christ" as a nine-year-old but won't talk about it now.

We focused on Jesse so much that we neglected our other kids, and Stacy and I neglected one another. Every time we were out on a so-called date, we talked about Jesse. And we blamed one another for Jesse's problems. I accused Stacy of being too easy on Jesse, and Stacy blamed me for being to harsh. The whole thing almost destroyed our marriage.

Though all four of Bob's kids grew up in the same environment, with the same values, only three excelled in school. Jesse struggled in the classroom, largely because of learning problems, and felt like a failure.

Many parents today put themselves under huge pressures to make sure their kids turn out all right. They take parenting extremely seriously, and I applaud that. But we must remember that one of the foremost parenting experts, James Dobson, teaches us to "focus on the family," not to "obsess on the family."

For example, some dads never miss their eight-year-olds' soccer games, critiquing every play of the game on the way home as the semi-interested kid finishes his snack from Tommy's mom, "who brings good treats." Some moms worry more about homework assignments than the kid does. Other parents are horrified if their kid scores lower than an "A-minus" because it hurts his chances of getting into a prestigious university. And what about parents who stay up late frantically typing their kid's mammal report or "helping" with a nature diorama while the kid plays video games in the other room?

Here's a dose of reality: Nothing you do will *guarantee* that your kid will grow up to be president of anything or become an NBA star or make the Olympics—or more importantly, follow the Lord as an adult. I appreciate your zeal to help your kids succeed, but you cannot guarantee that *they* will.

You're probably familiar with the proverb that says, "Train up a child in the way he should go, even when he is old, he will not depart from it" (22:6). Many parents mistakenly believe this proverb is a guarantee—God's promise that their children will turn out well. If it is a guarantee, it is surely not foolproof. Though Solomon wrote many proverbs, we're told that his son, Rehoboam, "forsook the law of the LORD" (2 Chronicles 12:1). We're also told that godly Eli, the priest, raised two sons who were "worthless men" and who extorted worshippers who came to sacrifice (see 1 Samuel 2).

Proverbs is a collection of valuable life lessons, but individual proverbs are *not* promises. The *Nelson New Illustrated Bible Commentary* says about Proverbs 22:6: "A godly parent has no guarantee from God for faithful children. Each generation is responsible for its own relationship with God. . . . There is no magic; there are no guarantees."

The *Believers Bible Commentary* says: "The usual interpretation of this proverb is that if you train up a child properly (in the way he should go), he will go on well in later life. Of course, there are exceptions."

"There are exceptions!" Sorry. So why try at all? I like the tongue-in-cheek quip from Lorne Sanny, former president of The Navigators: "Do the best you can at parenting, and when your kids turn 21, apologize to them." I like Sanny's honesty—a good starting point for parents of adult children.

Proverbs 22:6 is far from fatalistic. The word *train* means literally "to narrow." Parents must not abdicate their responsibility, letting adolescent minds do whatever they want (heaven forbid). We are responsible to "narrow" our children's values after God's. Chances are, they will follow those values when they are old—but it's no guarantee.

Also, Proverbs 22:6 tells us we are not to train our kids in the way *we want them to go* but in the way *they "should go."* How many parents demoralize their children by coercing them to be doctors, violinists, or preachers when they weren't meant to be those things? Only God has the right to choreograph your child's life. Only He bestows talents and sets the path.

Even after you have done all that Proverbs 22:6 suggests, your kids may still choose another way. Though you still love them, your heart is broken. And then there is guilt! Conscientious parents quickly blame themselves for wayward children. "If only" they had spent more quality time with this one or not been so strict with another. It's easy to blame yourself for your children's mistakes.

For our part, Alma and I know that we were not perfect parents, but we were faithful to do what we knew to do. Sure, we made errors, but we did more right than wrong. And we did seek God in helping us to train our children in the way they should go. We did our part faithfully if not perfectly.

That is true of Bob and Stacy as well. But there's still pain in parenting.

So why am I telling you this? Two reasons, I think, that might bring more realism to your parenting:

1. *Don't set yourself up for a big fall.* Even if you succeed 100 percent of the time at parenting, your children still have the capacity to make wrong choices. From the day they were born, you began preparing your children to be independent. Sometimes their choices are foolish, but you'll cripple them if you do not allow them freedom. Accepting the sobering possibility that children may not "turn out well" drives parents to their knees to pray. Instill deep biblical values for the long haul rather than merely trying to modify behavior.
2. *Watch for signs of "overparenting."* Parents naturally seek to protect their children from heartaches, but soon that

protective instinct insulates her from heartaches and isolates her from the real world. That agenda is different from the one used by the Lord, who uses suffering to build character. Overparenting can also prop up the sagging self-esteem of insecure parents as they see their children rise to the top of the class or hockey team. One TV advertisement for a phonics curriculum has a proud parent gushing to the TV camera, "My Gina is the best reader in her class." Nearly every parent would want to make that claim. But for whose gratification?

What is the issue here? It is partly an identity problem. Insecure dads relive their mediocre childhood sports careers through their promising twelve-year-olds. Moms project their dashed dream of becoming valedictorian through their bright eight-year-olds. Still, *overparenting* doesn't guarantee that your kid will *overachieve*. And frankly, it cripples the kid.

So strive to be a great parent, but realize that even God's first two children, Adam and Eve, made wrong choices. They did so despite having a perfect Parent, who honored them by giving them a free will.

Focus on doing *your job*—to parent faithfully—and insist your kids do *their job*. They need to do their own homework and school projects. Don't protect them from failure or they won't know how to cope with failure when it comes. And it will come. If they don't get into Harvard or win the Olympics, they might even turn out to be happier and more fulfilled. They might appreciate you more, too.

misconceptions about your body

you are what you look like

OUR NEWSPAPER RECENTLY RAN A story on what local celebrities dislike about their appearance, asking them, "If you could magically change one thing about your appearance, what would it be?" The celebrities' answers included higher cheekbones, a thinner body, no wrinkles, fuller lips, a thick head of hair, a smaller nose, and even a smaller head.

I appreciated their honesty. Over the last few decades, Americans have allowed skinny, airbrushed models on magazine covers at grocery checkout lines to become the standard for beauty. Who can measure up? And yet millions try.

Last year doctors in the United States performed nearly 8.5 million cosmetic procedures, including 177,000 nose jobs, 1.6 million Botox injections, and 215,000 breast augmentations.[1] Despite the psychological platitudes of countless books like *I'm Okay, You're Okay* and heartfelt self-acceptance exhortations from celebrities like Oprah Winfrey, people today still struggle to accept how they look. So have I.

My training in self-acceptance began when I was five. I remember playing the game "What do you like?" with an older cousin. (It was a silly game, I know, but we didn't have a TV.) First, I asked what foods he liked and then I moved to the "people category." It was a good-natured repartee, and his answer was always the same.

"Do you like your mom?" I quizzed.

"Yes, I like my mom."

"Do you like Aunt Sally?"

"Yes, I like Aunt Sally," he replied patiently with a smile.

As the game went on, I couldn't find anybody he didn't like. Finally, without thinking I asked, "Do you like yourself?"

"Do I like myself?" he repeated. He paused. "No, not very much."

I was shocked. I was only five, but I knew that was not a good answer. How could you not like yourself?

I found out as a teenager.

During our early years my dad gave his three sons haircuts while we sat on a metal stool in our farmhouse kitchen. He made a joke of asking what style we wanted, but we knew it was going to be a buzz cut. Dad acquired his training from shearing our three sheep, which, as far as he was concerned, was easier than working on his boys. Sheep were less squirmy, and he earned a few bucks selling the wool. Also, he didn't have to clip the sheep once a month.

The mirror in the kitchen was only six feet away, but no one was allowed to look until Dad finished. It didn't matter if you liked your hair or not. You were stuck with the cut until next month.

Finally, when I turned thirteen, I was allowed to go to Curly's barbershop below the bank. My first store-bought haircut! Right away I noticed a huge mirror covering the south wall. While Curly (who was bald as a cue ball) cut my hair, I stared into that mirror and studied my appearance—and Curly's.

Curly was smooth and handsome. And so it seemed was everyone else in the shop. Except me. My head was the size of a prize-winning watermelon. You could see it even in the baby picture hanging in our living room: goofy one-year-old Scott smiling into the camera with his balloon head! Mom had told me all babies have oversized heads, but I suspected she was just trying to make me feel good.

At Curly's, my suspicions were confirmed. My head *was* too big. And my ears stuck out. At that moment, I didn't like myself very much.

It wasn't until my twenties that my perception began to change. As

I read the biblical account of creation, my confidence grew: "And God saw all that He had made, and behold, *it was very good*" (Genesis 1:31, emphasis added). *God doesn't make trash,* I realized. *He created me exactly the way He intended—melon head and all.*

I also discovered Psalm 139, which says, "For You formed my inward parts; You wove me in my mother's womb" (verses 13–14). I decided I needed to see my body from God's perspective rather than mine. If God accepted me, then I should accept myself.

It's so easy to revert to the world's standards, though. Recently one morning after getting out of bed, I stood in front of the mirror and commented on how unattractive I felt. Alma calmly reminded me that in our house, we were not to make deprecating statements about anyone—including ourselves! After all, we're created in God's image. But I felt so ugly! *Never mind,* I told myself. *God's truth trumps feelings—even in front of the mirror. Let it go.*

So how does this principle work for someone born with partially formed limbs or fused fingers? Though it seems simplistic, I don't believe I'm being naïve when I say the answer is the same. Sure, surgery can fix some problems, but unless we accept ourselves at our core, our only alternative is railing in anger at the Creator or drifting into bitterness. We must realize we are more than our bodies—even when our bodies are "imperfect."

Still, as Scripture says, our bodies are temples, and we ought to take care of these "temples" God has given us. That's practicing good stewardship. But comparing ourselves to others and obsessing about how poorly we think we look is like telling God He goofed!

In his book *The Inflated Self,* David Myers tells the story of Pinocchio, the puppet who struggled with low self-esteem. Finally, he turns to Gepetto, his maker, and says, "Papa, I'm not sure who I am, but if I'm alright with you, then I guess I'm alright with me!"

What would you like to magically change about your appearance? Whatever it is, let it go. Your Maker has said you are "alright with Him," so you are truly all right.

denial is the best way to handle aging

ARE YOU AGING WELL? I'M NOT. Although I'm better at it now, I've found it hard to admit I'm getting older.

Take birthdays for example. When I turned twenty-five, Alma found me at the breakfast table holding my head in my hands and repeating sadly, "I'm a quarter of a century old. A quarter of a century old!" When I turned thirty, my wide-eyed daughters found me sitting on the ledge of our fireplace muttering, "I'm thirty years old. . . . I'm thirty years old. . . ." They just rolled their eyes as they hustled off to school.

Norman Corwin quipped in *The Ageless Spirit* that the toughest birthday he ever faced was his fortieth, "because it said good-bye, good-bye, and good-bye to youth." I, too, had to bid adieu to my youth in my early forties when my muscles got stiff after a ballgame with my son and the neighborhood kids. Soon even the whirly-dippy carnival rides at the state fair gave me nausea.

Then I was "attacked" by a kidney stone early one June morning after spending the previous day working in the yard. "Your body is like a machine that needs replacement parts," my doctor told me. "You're not going to live forever." (Thanks, Doc!)

I also realized I could relate to jokes about aging. For instance, you know you are old when someone tells you the details about his last surgery and you're actually interested. Or when you need your glasses to find your glasses. Or when you frequent restaurants only on the days they give senior discounts.

The older we get, the faster the days seem to fly by. Even Job lamented, "My days are swifter than a weaver's shuttle" (Job 7:6).

American culture tells us that we must preserve our youth and avoid aging at all costs. In our society, for instance, it is impolite to ask an adult his or her age — especially *her* age. "Thirty-nine and holding" is a common answer. This attitude is everywhere, even among Christians. A Christian ad agency I know announces staff members' birthdays during its monthly meeting. Each time, the employees proudly share the day of their birth but joke about not divulging the year.

It's time to denounce the insidious Western worldview that aging is bad. In Asia and Africa, the elderly are revered! Rather than buy into our society's view of aging, I suggest we embrace three universal truths:

First, we are all "terminal." As President William McKinley lay dying of an assassin's bullet, his loving wife cried, "I want to go too! I want to go too!" McKinley replied, "You will, my dear. You will." Life insurance salespeople joke that there is a 100 percent chance we will die. But it took me years — not until I was in my forties — to realize that I was terminal. Even then I didn't think the grim reaper would show up for a thousand years or so. I couldn't imagine not being around.

Second, your age does not determine who you are as a person. You may not be able to go on carnival rides without hurling, but you are still of great value! You may not be able to work as hard in your career or accomplish as much around the house, but that doesn't mean you're insignificant. A fifty-something-year-old missionary friend of mine understood this well. In her final days she lay dying of cancer, unable to get out of bed and barely able to speak. Despite her frailty, she radiated strength to those around her. "I am more than my body," she would say with conviction.

Third, death is not the end — it is simply a point of transition.

The Bible says we are eternal beings and that our souls live on after our physical bodies wither away. Robert Moffat, a Christian leader who traveled extensively in the early 1900s raising funds for the YMCA, said that death would simply be where he "changed trains." Well said.

The Bible also has some encouraging words about the aging process. The apostle Paul put the American view in perspective, writing, "Therefore we do not lose heart, but though our outer man is decaying, yet our inner man is being renewed day by day" (2 Corinthians 4:16).

Paul would have agreed with William McKinley: we *are* going to die. We may spend millions at health clubs to slow down the process, but we can't stop the decay. So what will it be—Bally's or the Bible? I choose the Bible, of course! Paul said in 1 Timothy 4:8 that bodily exercise offers "little profit, but godliness is profitable for all things." Our inner person must be our priority. (I'll keep my gym membership, though, because my body houses the Holy Spirit and I want to be a good landlord!)

May I ask you a question? Are you tempted to believe that youth is everything and aging is to be avoided? If so, you'll feel more worthless with each passing birthday.

Instead of focusing on my age, I try to live out the following principles:

- I will be grateful each morning for another day. I could have died in my sleep.
- I will not complain about aging, for when I die I will continue on in the presence of the Lord.
- I won't wait until I am retired to live out my dreams.
- I will stay in reasonable physical shape so I can wrestle with my grandchildren.
- Above all, I will commit to developing my inner person every day. I'll take time for prayer, solitude, Bible meditation, fasting, reading, fellowship, and sharing with others.

Incidentally, I wrote this chapter on my sixtieth birthday. And I did not sit at the kitchen table, holding my head and repeating sadly, "I'm sixty years old." Instead, I said proudly to everyone who wished me happy birthday, "I'm sixty!"

How old are you?

no heaven-bound person should be afraid of dying

IN THE 1940S AND 1950S, MY former boss, Rod Sargent, was mentored by Dawson Trotman, founder of The Navigators. Rod had walked with God for more than thirty years by the time I started working with him. But he soon developed cancer—for the second time. He had courageously fought it ten years earlier, but now it was back with a vengeance. I remember once walking by his office in mid-afternoon, seeing him with his head down on his desk, so great was the pain. But that year, as we continued to work together and his strength slowly ebbed, this man of God mentored me.

During one of our visits, I asked how he felt. "Fine," he said. He wasn't fine—he just didn't want to talk about his illness.

Then there was a silence. Seeing an opening to learn about his faith, I sheepishly asked, "Do you fear death?"

"No, I don't fear death," he answered quietly, "but I fear the *process* of death."

I nodded my head, but I didn't get it. How could I? I was barely forty. I still felt invincible.

When Rod was no longer able to come to the office, I went to his home to work on direct-mail copy. During those interviews he never complained, but it was painful to watch him. He couldn't get comfortable in his chair. He fidgeted and grimaced. Our appointments became shorter and shorter until I finally began going upstairs to his bed to talk with him amid the surgical tubing.

Not only was his body slipping away, but his steel-trap mind was also showing cracks from all the pain medication. Once, he agreed to draft a longhand letter for me to pick up. Rod handed me the paper as I stood at his bedside.

"You'd better take it from here," he said sadly. He had scrawled only two sentences before the writing trailed away.

Rod knew he was losing his faculties. Still, each week he smiled graciously and gave me his undivided attention. My visits now lasted only a few minutes.

That winter I had planned a weekend trip to Phoenix, but I sensed that I should speak to Rod first. Stopping by his house the day before I left town, I blubbered out what had been on my heart for months.

"Rod. . .I, um, just wanted to say something," I began. "I want you to know I appreciate your attention to detail. In your writing and in general. You may not realize it, but you've done a lot for me, and I, uh, just wanted to tell you that I'm grateful."

It wasn't eloquent, and I could barely keep from crying. I had no idea I'd be so emotional. Rod smiled and thanked me.

It was my last memory of him. He died Sunday while I was away. I don't know if my words were encouraging, but I'm glad I took the initiative to talk with him. That last visit with Rod reminds me of the old saying:

If you think the credit's due him,
Now's the time to slip it to him,
For he cannot read his tombstone
When he's dead.

Now that I've had a few more birthdays and a few more aches and pains, I understand what Rod said about fearing the process of death. Film director Woody Allen quipped, "I know I'm going to die. I just don't want to be there when it happens."

But death is not as simple as that. Unlike Woody Allen, I *do* want to be there—but I'd rather not be around for the painful weeks, months, or years that may lead up to my death. I'm not much good at being sick. Hospitals and illness give me the willies, despite the great care of the hardworking, conscientious people in the medical profession. Then again, who says I'm going to die a slow arduous death? Perhaps I'll get hit by a runaway beer truck as I jaywalk! Or maybe I'll die in my sleep. Or have a brain hemorrhage during extra innings at a Colorado Rockies ballgame.

Of course, speculating about how I will die is not my job. Those details belong to God. Years later, I spoke with another ailing friend who was also mentored by Dawson Trotman—the late Lorne Sanny, who succeeded Trotman as president of The Navigators. Lorne had also been stricken with cancer, and the two of us were discussing his future.

Lorne smiled. "Today, I'm doing fine, but Psalm 31:15 helps me when I worry." He quoted, "My times are in Your hand; deliver me from the hand of my enemies and from those who persecute me."

Then he explained the Hebrew word for "times" can be translated *terminus*. "Terminus means 'the end,'" Lorne said. "God decides when it is time for my life to end—not only when but how. I trust Him for the *when* and the *how*. And I hope that if I leave slowly, my last hours will be sharing Christ by word or action to a nurse or medical attendant."

What a perspective! Lorne did not candy-coat the process of death, but he faced it with a godly perspective.

I've concluded that if the Creator was wise in His timing of creating me, is He now unwise in how He has arranged my terminus? He is either altogether wise or He is not. Though none of us wants to endure a painful death, we can trust that the One who loved us enough to bring us into the world will love us still as He takes us home—in His timing and in His way.

One more thing: do you need to give someone—a friend, family member, or colleague—a heartfelt commendation on a life well lived? Do it now. Don't wait until Sunday.

misconceptions about generally accepted rules

tithing is the standard

A LEX AND I MET EVERY TWO weeks at 7:00 a.m. to read the Bible at his modest, seven hundred square-foot duplex. Before he believed in Christ, Alex, by his own admission, had done his share of drinking and carousing. But beneath his wild living was a gentle, honest man who was seeking God. God richly blessed me as Alex and I became friends. After we read the Gospel of John together for eight months, he humbly turned to Christ. Praise to God!

Alex knew little about the teachings of the church. He was eager to grow spiritually, though, and he would beam when he was able to find books in the Bible without me giving him the page number. We both were delighted when he discovered a storefront church near his home. There, he found a warm spiritual family and was baptized.

Then one Tuesday morning, Alex "popped" the question. "Last Sunday the pastor preached on tithing," he began. "Said everyone in the church needs to tithe. That's 10 percent, right?"

"Ten percent," I echoed.

Alex winced. "I don't know. I want to obey the Lord, but. . ."

I thought it best to keep quiet. I knew where this was going.

He continued, "Okay, I take home $800 a month. If I tithe, that leaves me $720, and my rent is $550."

I glanced around the tiny but comfortable room.

Alex was talking louder now. "That leaves $170 for groceries for me and two kids" — his wife was long gone — "not to mention gas for the car, paying the babysitter, clothes, and we sure better not get sick!"

He paused. "I can't afford to tithe, can I?"

I waited.

Alex went on, "But the pastor said that if we trust God, He will make it up to us. He said we should give by faith, whether we can afford it or not. Bring all the tithe into the storehouse and God will open a window of blessing."

"Malachi 3:10," I offered.

Alex nodded. "What do you think? Should I give 10 percent and trust the Lord for gas money so I can get to work? Will God make it up to me?"

What would you have answered Alex? I didn't know what to say. I believe strongly in generous giving, but Alex's budget gave me second thoughts. I couldn't ignore the pain in his eyes. *Maybe tithing is only for the upper middle class,* I thought.

Two weeks later, I was studying the Bible with another friend. This one lived in a new, four thousand-square-foot home in a gated community. Unlike Alex, Rex had been a believer for a long time and was equally dedicated to growing in his walk with God.

As I passed through Rex's heavy ornamental gate after our Bible study, I reflected on the issue of tithing again. If Rex's take-home income was $200,000 per year and he tithed 10 percent, he would still have $180,000 on which to eke out a living. That's when I convinced myself that the 10-percent standard is too simplistic.

Then I thought about Luke 21:1-4. You may know the story. Jesus was at the temple, watching the rich place their offerings into urns. He also saw a "certain poor widow putting in two small copper coins. And He said, 'Truly I say to you, this poor widow put in more than all of them; for they all out of their surplus put into the offering; but she out of her poverty put in all that she had to live on.'"

All she had? Did she give her entire asset base? Many Bible scholars think not, because that would contradict Old Testament proverbs about planning ahead and leaving an inheritance. It's instructive to remember that in those days, laborers were paid at the end of each workday as they left the landlord's field. I believe that's the money the widow sacrificially gave—all she had to live on *that day.*

The rich worshippers may have contributed more total money than the widow, but measured by Jesus' yardstick, the widow gave more. Why? Because she gave out of her "living," not out of her surplus. What was important to Jesus was not the amount but the cost.

Also, notice what Jesus did not say: He could have taught on traditional tithing, but He did not! He could have quoted Malachi 3:10 about bringing "the whole tithe into the storehouse," but He did not!

Tithing is mentioned in passing only twice in the New Testament—in Matthew 23:23 and Luke 11:42, which both refer to the same incident, and in Luke 18:12. Yet today, giving 10 percent is considered the standard.

Is this standard being kept? The IRS reports that American taxpayers give 1 to 2 percent of their gross income to charity—a figure that has not changed in thirty years. Because evangelicals make up approximately half the population, shouldn't the giving rate be higher?

A recent Barna study showed that 75 percent of Americans give to their church in a typical month and nearly 90 percent contribute annually. However, the median given per year is $500 to their church and $750 total to charity of any kind. Barna's conclusion: "Believers frequently donate money to their church—but they don't donate very much." The organization estimates that just 8 percent of all Christians tithe (10 percent).[1]

I suppose if I were a pastor faced with this discouraging news I would lean on my congregation to give 10 percent, too. But although tithing is commendable, I don't believe the Bible commands it for New Testament believers. Ten percent is too little for some and too unrealistic for others.

So how about an alternative? Instead of traditional tithing, try something more in tune with the spirit of Luke 21: give in such a way that it makes a huge dent in your lifestyle. It's a subjective way to view giving, but it's freeing. Think about it. If our giving does not alter our other financial decisions, is it truly "Luke 21" style giving?

The Old Testament tells the story of King David, who tried to buy a threshing floor from Araunah to erect an altar to the Lord (2 Samuel 24:18-25). Good-hearted Araunah offered it for free and added oxen for the sacrifice as well. But David demurred, "I will not offer burnt offerings to the LORD my God which cost me nothing" (verse 24).

Does your giving dent your lifestyle? Or do you make lifestyle choices first with giving as an afterthought?

Asking these questions year after year will cause you to reexamine your stewardship decisions—and that's good. You might end up simplifying your life. Do you really need to own twenty-seven sport-coats, subscribe to five outerwear catalogs, and drive three cars?

Thinking "sacrifice" instead of "tithe" may take some getting used to, but it's the best way to answer the difficult question of how much you should give. C. S. Lewis implies that biblical charity is giving more than what you can afford to do without anyway. And specifically, "I am afraid the only safe rule is to give more than we can spare."[2]

Shouldn't generosity cost you something?

skipping church is no big deal

'VE HEARD LOTS OF BELIEVERS lament, "I get more out of staying home and reading my Bible than attending church." In fact, many *committed* Christians say this! Sadly, I've said it, too. I confess that there was a period in my life when I stayed home on Sunday mornings to read my Bible, go to the swamp to bird watch, or just take it easy. I'm not proud that I skipped church, but I did. And sometimes I'm still tempted to have Sunday morning sleep-ins.

I'm not alone. According to pollster George Barna, only 63 percent of born-again believers attended a worship service last week. Furthermore, he states, "In a typical worship service, about half claim that they did not experience God's presence or feel that they interacted with Him in a personal way." Barna concludes, "Less than one quarter of all born-again adults consciously strive to make worship part of their lifestyle."[1] As blues man B. B. King says, "the thrill is gone!" That seems to be true for 75 percent of evangelicals. Why? Here are a few possibilities.

First, fatigue. Many of us are so worn down Monday through Saturday that we dread Sunday, especially if we have to lug an eighteen-pound diaper bag to the nursery, monitor the street attire of our teenage daughter, or see to it that our spouse looks decent ("You're not wearing that, are you?"). If you have responsibilities, such as teaching squirrelly fourth graders, handling the offering, or singing in the choir, Sunday seems like a stormy Monday rather than a day of rest.

My friends Damon and Suzie from Minneapolis used to say that Sunday was the worst day of their week—and they're dedicated believers! By the time they got three energetic kids and a colicky baby into the car, all six family members were crabby. Damon said, "When we walked into the building, we were in no shape to worship God!" Feeling guilty, he resorted to leading the family in singing hymns in the car in order to get their attitudes right before entering God's holy house.

I admire their honesty. I can identify! After silently cursing the convoy of cheerful Minnesota boaters nonchalantly using *my* road to get to their favorite lake, I would walk into church feeling cranky. And my bad mood would intensify when I met those overly extroverted greeters at the door. Bah humbug!

A second reason we skip church is we disagree with the way things are handled. I've sat in the pew and grumbled:

"Why have we been singing the same three-word chorus for fifteen minutes? I want something with a little more meat. Can't we just sing 'Amazing Grace' like Jesus' disciples did?

"Why are the announcements so long? We could be outta here two minutes earlier if they would just print the information in the bulletin. Can't the handbell choir read their own practice schedule?

"Why do they let that guy sing solos? He's flat.

"How come we don't worship with guitars and drums like other churches do?

"Who picked the color of this carpet?"

Like consumers, we as believers are looking for the perfect church—one that will satisfy our every need. But like Howard Hendricks of Dallas Seminary is fond of saying, "If you find the perfect church, don't join it or it won't be perfect!"

Another reason we'd rather stay home is because of the people. I admit I get annoyed at those who come primarily to exchange business

skipping church is no big deal

cards, who whisper during hymns, or who sneeze into their hands just before we exchange greetings. I know I'm being critical, but I've heard others say the same.

So where have we gone wrong? Is it that we start off on the wrong foot by considering worship a spectator sport. We go to church Sunday morning with the same attitude we had twelve hours earlier at a Saturday night ball game. Entertain me! Show me a good time! Make sure I get something out of it! Meet my needs or I'm not coming back!

Sundays began to change for me when I began to see corporate worship as a spiritual discipline—one in which I focused on giving, not getting. As I did with other spiritual disciplines, I learned to make corporate worship a habit.

Yes, sometimes it's a hassle to get there on time. Yes, some elements of the service can be goofy. And some of the people bug me. But I've dropped my judgmental attitude. Today, I simply refuse to criticize what I see at the worship service. Period. Dozens of others may feel called to criticize the pastor or the music or the extroverted ushers, but I do not.

I can't ignore this passage from Hebrews 10:24-25: "And let us consider how to stimulate one another to love and good deeds, not forsaking our own assembling together, as is the habit of some, but encouraging one another; and all the more, as you see the day drawing near."

As I have changed my attitude from critical spectator to cooperative participant—from taker to giver—I *do* meet God in corporate worship. Rarely do I get misty eyed in my personal devotions, but it is rare that I am not deeply moved during Sunday services.

If goofy practices are keeping you away, speak up to the proper people in a humble way. But don't use it as an excuse to attend Bedside Baptist. Is there a law that says you must go every Sunday? No. No more than there is a law that says you must have a quiet time every day. But what if you do get more out of Sunday morning by staying home with your Bible, blueberry bagels, and a TV preacher? Maybe you need to change churches. Or maybe you need to rearrange your week so you are not ready to collapse by Sunday. Or maybe you need to change your outlook. Ask the Lord to help you identify why assembling with your forever family is such a drag.

CHAPTER 34

God expects 110 percent

M Y BASEBALL COACH AT IOWA STATE was L. C. "Cap" Timm. Cap was a wise man, clean shaven as Division I college coaches often are. He played minor-league ball as a catcher and had the broken body parts to prove it. His nose seemed to be in two parts, with some of it straight and the tip folded neatly to the right at a ninety-degree angle. His ever-present thick glasses rested on his nose comfortably. His nose wasn't unattractive, just crooked.

His fingers also were crooked—the result of foul tips. He couldn't straighten most of them. His right pinkie, in fact, extended just forty-five degrees. While in the military, Cap was ordered by his commanding officer to straighten his fingers so he could give a proper salute. "That's the best I can do, sir," he replied. After that Cap was reassigned to the Army's baseball program, where broken-fingered salutes were acceptable.

I only heard him yell at a ballplayer once, and that was the day a highly touted sophomore threw his bat after a disappointing round in the batting cage. Sixty-five-year-old Cap ripped off his Coke-bottle glasses and grabbed the muscular kid by the shirt. "You wanna fight right here, right now?" Cap shouted, glaring at the angry sophomore.

I too was highly touted, with an ego to match. As a left-handed pitcher, my strength was a nasty fastball that tailed away from righties if it didn't hit them first. I put everything I had into every pitch — 110 percent.

Cap liked the nasty fastball, but he urged me to pitch 90 percent. Why? He had two reasons: first, with overexertion the ball often flattened out and wouldn't tail. Second, he wanted me to learn control — it's harder to throw strikes at 110 percent.

I understood his point about strikes. I often struck out over a dozen batters but walked nine or ten! Once in a while, though, I could throw 110 percent and still maintain control. With that little success, I resisted Cap's 90 percent doctrine. Some games I determined to throw 90 percent, but ego and adrenaline urged me to throw harder and harder, especially with major league scouts in the stands.

I should have learned this lesson against Nebraska my senior year, the year the Baltimore Orioles drafted me. I felt particularly strong that day, but the harder I threw, the harder the Cornhuskers ripped line drives. Cap didn't take me out of the game. He was waiting for me to ease back, but I didn't. The first inning must have lasted an hour, and by the time it was over I had given up eight runs.

Why am I telling you this? Because some people make the mistake of putting 110 percent into everything they do. I discovered after I stopped playing baseball that I was living the way I pitched. No matter how many hours I put in at the office it wasn't enough. I thought constantly about getting more sales and beating last year's quota.

Even in ministry I gave 110 percent. I found myself getting up early and going to bed later because I thought the work would not succeed without my heroic efforts. But I was tired, and success was eluding me.

The turning point came late one night after I'd spent yet another long evening in ministry. Though it was midnight, I flopped on the sofa and opened my Bible randomly to Psalm 127. I was shocked at verse two: "It is vain for you to rise up early, to retire late, to eat the bread of painful labors; for He gives to His beloved even in his sleep."

I couldn't believe it. God blesses us, His beloved, while we sleep? I figured God would bless me only when I gave 110 percent. What was I missing?

Tentatively, I started working reasonable hours. I spent unhurried time alone reading the Bible and praying rather than racing out for early-morning appointments. I spent more time with my kids and didn't answer the phone in the middle of playtime.

Irresponsible? No, I still worked hard, but I didn't *overwork*. I tried to work faithfully, not frantically.

I can't tell you that I noticed a dramatic change, but I can tell you I was happier—and not so tired. Although I scheduled fewer appointments, our ministry to college students grew from ten to seventy-five. Although I cut my hours at the newspaper, I still earned warm commendations from my boss—not only for my sales performance but also for infecting the office with "enthusiasm," as he called it.

I can also tell you that people noticed a change. Those who worked with me in ministry enjoyed it more because I wasn't so uptight. I hadn't realized how much pressure I had put on others.

I realized my thinking was changing the night the band "Hot Tuna" was performing on campus. It was the same night as our weekly student discipleship gathering. Instead of going directly to our meeting, I meandered through the field house where the band was setting up. The air was already blue with various kinds of illegal smoke. Soon ten thousand screaming Iowa Hawkeyes would attend this concert. I was nervous, hoping that we might attract even fifty or sixty students at our meeting two hundred yards away across the quad. Then I realized the success of the event didn't depend on me. As the psalmist said, "He gives to His beloved even in his sleep" (127:2).

That night God infused me with new confidence as I taught the Bible to sixty students who wanted to follow Christ, including some new believers who, the year before, probably would have been getting high with "Hot Tuna."

How I wish I had followed the advice of Cap Timm sooner, both in baseball and in life! Just as it was a step of faith to throw a baseball at 90 percent, so now it is a step of faith to go to bed at a decent hour after a faithful day's service and count on the Lord to work even while I sleep.

I'm not suggesting halfhearted effort. Some of us need to go from 60 percent to 90 percent! But overachievers need to check out Psalm 127:2. And note the word *beloved.*

Today when I hear TV sports commentators gush, "That ballplayer gives 110 percent," I smile and think of Cap with his Coke-bottle glasses, crooked nose, and broken fingers.

Now I get it.

CHAPTER 35

God's will is tough to figure out

CHECK OUT ANY CHRISTIAN CONFERENCE, AND most likely you'll find a workshop titled "How to Find the Will of God." Believers migrate toward that topic like mosquitoes to a Wisconsin fish-boil, hoping to answer questions like:

- What career should I pursue?
- Should I take a job promotion and move to a new city?
- Which church should I attend?
- Shall I remodel the kitchen? (Or, now that I've started remodeling, how do I get my spouse to talk to me again?)

We also want to know God's will on smaller matters, such as:

- Which gym should I join?
- What outfit shall I wear?
- Should I fill up my car with regular or premium gas?

To help answer these types of questions, seminar presenters provide ways in which believers can find God's will. They suggest letting the Holy Spirit, God's Word, and the counsel of godly friends lead you. Giving your biases and desires to God and waiting. Following your heart.

Even with all this information, believers today still have two huge misconceptions about finding God's will. The first is that the goal of walking with God is to find His will for our life. Scripture, however, implies that knowledge of God's will is a *byproduct* of seeking God: "But seek first His kingdom and His righteousness; and all these things shall be added to you" (Matthew 6:33). Christ's followers are to be preoccupied with His kingdom and His righteousness—not with discovering our life's road map. As we spend our energy living faithfully in His kingdom, knowing the King's plan for us will follow.

Similarly, when the apostle Paul met Christ on the road to Damascus, he asked two questions: "Who are You, Lord?" and "What do You want me to do?"

The order is important. First, know the Lord. Second, know His will. A minor distinction? I don't think so. It may seem like a noble task to find God's will for my life, but if it is the focus of my relationship with Christ, I become terribly self-centered. Jesus becomes my celestial decision-maker, not the lover of my soul. So relax. Seek the kingdom. You'll be unable to avoid God's will.

The second misconception many believers have is that God guides us without our having to make risky decisions. Think of it this way. When children are young, their parents make most decisions for them—what they eat, what they wear, what time they go to bed. Unfortunately, nowadays many parents ask their two-year-olds what they want for dinner, what they want to wear, and when they want to go to bed. If you have already determined the dinner menu, why invite an argument with someone who wants cheese and Jell-O for every meal?

I digress.

As children grow older, parents encourage them to make their own decisions on small issues first, then on larger ones. For instance, when your daughter is young, you ask her whether she would like to wear her red dress to school or her blue pants with the pretty flowers. But when she's sixteen, you don't dictate what she should wear. Instead, you say, "You're not going to school in that, are you?" And if your twenty-six-year-old asks what she should wear to the accounting office tomorrow, you let her decide. Since you have taught her your values, you have confidence she will make wise choices.

I've talked with many believers who say that finding God's will seems more difficult now than it was when they were new believers. They say God clearly guided them in those early days, but they don't sense His divine direction anymore.

Maybe God guides us the way we guide our children. As we mature, we begin thinking the way He thinks. We love what He loves and disdain what He disdains. He entrusts more and more decisions to us because He is building His values in us.

God reveals His methods of guidance in the Psalms, saying, "I will instruct you and teach you in the way which you should go; I will counsel you with my eye upon you. Do not be as the horse or as the mule which have no understanding, whose trapping include bit and bridle to hold them in check" (Psalm 32:8-9). He promises to instruct us, but we are not to be like a non-thinking horse, which gets direction from the bit and bridle. The Lord expects us to use our discernment rather than wait mindlessly for an obvious tug or nudge.

The book of Isaiah continues in this vein, saying, "Your ears will hear a word behind you, 'This is the way, walk in it,' whenever you turn to the right or to the left" (30:21). Notice the timing. God will lead us *whenever* or *as* we are turning—not before. God will guide as you decide. Sure, it's riskier than waiting for that open door, but we need to trust His methods of parenting. This honors Him!

There's a catch, though.

This principle is predicated upon our doing His general will. That includes loving our neighbors, living out the fruit of the Spirit, and rejoicing in the Lord when we'd rather whine. In short, living like a kingdom dweller ought to. And that brings us back to Matthew 6:33—seeking first His kingdom.

Too many Christians emphasize the specific will of God (my neighborhood gym or the YMCA?), but they forget that the general will of God comes first. For example, asking God to guide you to someone with whom you could have a sexual affair violates the general will of God (the seventh commandment). God will not give you specific guidance because the inquiry is out of line.

As you focus on Paul's first question, "Who are You, Lord?" you'll find yourself responding to issues the same way God does. When that happens, you'll be getting closer to where God will honor *your* choices.

Martin Luther said, "Love God and do as you please." Surprise! Now, how will you handle all that freedom?

misconceptions about integrity

your outer life dictates your character

HARDLY A DAY PASSES WITHOUT A news headline about a powerful person who did something stupid. For example, this summer our newspaper reported: basketball star Kobe Bryant commits adultery. Communications giant Qwest executives are accused of fraud. Baseball star Sammy Sosa corks a bat to improve his average. Accounting firm Arthur Andersen admits to "misreporting" Enron's profits.

But the report that I found most distressing was from my alma mater, Iowa State University. There, head basketball coach Larry Eustachy was fired because of his drinking binges and partying with coeds after Big 12 games. To his credit, he admitted his mistake and sought treatment. Still, it crushed me to know one of our own could do such a thing. When Mike Tyson or someone from California screws up, it seems far away and almost expected — but not in Iowa!

I have not yet read today's paper. But in a few minutes, when I glance through the sports and business sections, I'm confident I will find a celebrity who was picked up for DUI, caught in a sexual affair, or bit the ear off an opponent. And that's before I turn to national news!

These public figures repeat a common excuse. "I never intended to be a role model," they say. "I just want to put this behind me." Enough! Let's call it what it is — lack of integrity. Let's admit it: The world of sports and business focuses more on looking good externally than on building internal integrity.

While it's easy to chide celebrities, are you and I all that different? Imagine if the headlines read like these:

- "Church Secretary and Pastor Flirt Behind Closed Doors"
- "Christian Employee Charges Mileage for Personal Errands"
- "Sunday School Teacher Given Too Much Change by Mistake—Keeps It"
- "Missionary Caught Ogling Neighbor's Wife"
- "Bible Study Leader Calls in Sick to Go Shopping"

None of these offenses would land us in jail, but don't these little wrongs signal a lack of integrity? Did the Enron cheaters start by misreporting millions or by "reinterpreting" minor tax laws? Did the pastor's sexual indiscretion start by watching "harmless" soft porn?

It's my guess that these public figures began with fudging little things—just like you and I are tempted to do. Luke 16:10 says, "He who is faithful in a very little thing is faithful also in much; and he who is unrighteous in a very little thing is unrighteous also in much." Little things matter because they reveal our below-the-surface integrity.

When I think of internal below-the-surface integrity, a farming term comes to mind: "tamping" fence posts. If you don't know what tamping fence posts means, hang on.

Each June, my brothers and I set out with our dad on a quest to put up eighty rods of woven wire hog fence. My dad drilled the postholes about a rod apart (16 ½ feet) from the comfort of our John Deere "B" tractor, which came complete with an umbrella to keep away the hot Iowa sun. Easy job.

My two brothers rolled out the woven wire next to the holes Dad was drilling, then dropped fence posts into the three-foot-deep holes from a flatbed wagon pulled slowly along by an "M" John Deere. Easy job.

My job was the hard one—tamping in the posts, leaving them straight and firm so the hogs could not push them over. My dad equipped me with weighted eight-foot metal tamping pipe two inches in diameter. With it, I tamped down the dirt around the posts. The tamping pipe weighed fifteen pounds at 8:00 a.m. and sixty-five pounds at 4:00 p.m.

The eighty posts seemed to stretch out to the horizon like a single-file row of pine trees. I figured the hogs would die of old age before I finished. But Dad trained me well. "An inch at the bottom is worth a foot at the top," he would tell me. Meaning, pack the dirt tightly at the bottom, and as you get closer to the surface the soil won't need to be tamped as tightly. He demonstrated, taking his time to tamp solidly at the bottom, leaving messy little piles of dirt lying on the surface when he stopped. Then he punched the post with his gloved fist. It pinged like a tuning fork—straight and sturdy. He smiled and handed me the tamper. Only seventy-nine to go!

After four posts, my arms ached. It took forever to tamp just one post. It seemed to me that the posts would be tighter and the job would go faster if they were firmly tamped at the top. Why compact the soil at the bottom where it wasn't visible anyway?

So I experimented. I pushed dirt into the hole without tamping until I got to the top. Then I tamped vigorously. The job went much faster and the post appeared as sturdy as the others. There wasn't any loose dirt lying around either. Proud of my discovery, I concluded I was smarter than Dad.

Just in case, though, I gave the post a gentle push. At once my sturdy post fell sideways. Horrified, I straightened it and tamped furiously again at the top. There, straight and firm. I nudged it again. Again, it gave way easily. Disappointed, I got on my knees and laboriously dug the dirt out of the hole with my bare hands; then I applied Dad's "inch at the bottom" rule. I nudged the post. Solid!

Building strong character is similar. Do we focus on looking good on the surface? Or are we "tamping" below? Tamping at the bottom takes time — and so does building integrity. Like my hastily top-tamped fence post, many people today can be easily toppled when the pressure is on.

Jesus would have liked Dad's "inch at the bottom" principle. In Matthew 7, He tells the story of one homebuilder who built his house upon solid rock and another foolish one who built his house on sand. Both houses looked equally strong until the "rain came down, the streams rose, and the winds blew and beat against that house [built on sand], and it fell with a great crash" (verse 27, NIV).

An inch at the bottom is worth a foot at the top.

financial decisions are not spiritual decisions

WE GO TO A SMALL DRY-CLEANING store on the other side of town run by an American and his Korean wife. Unlike the dry cleaners in our neighborhood, they actually iron creases in the proper places, not in the general area where creases ought to be. Though it takes twenty minutes and we pass other cleaning establishments on the way, it's worth the drive.

Having spent seven weeks in Seoul years ago, the trip gives me the opportunity to practice the three words of Korean I know—hello, good-bye, and baseball. The Korean lady smiles and congratulates me on my language proficiency. Then I can't resist commenting on Korea's staple food, kimchee, cabbage soaked in hot spices for two or three decades. American passports should be stamped "No Kimchee!"

I digress.

About a year ago when I brought my dry cleaning home, I noticed a small plastic bag with the store logo suspended from a hanger. Inside was a twenty-five-cent piece—they had found a quarter in one of my pockets.

I held the quarter in my hands. I would never have missed it. But despite serving hundreds of customers, the dry cleaners went to the trouble to put my twenty-five cents into a bag and return it. Amazing. I could understand Abraham Lincoln doing this in 1840 when a quarter was worth something, but today? Why do such a thing? I intended to ask the following week.

In the last chapter I quoted Luke 16:10, which describes the importance of exercising faithfulness in little things. Fail in the little things and you'll fail in big issues too. But verses 11 and 12 are often overlooked. "If therefore you have not been faithful in the use of unrighteous mammon, who will entrust the true riches to you? And if you have not been faithful in the use of that which is another's, who will give you that which is your own?"

Jesus says the way we handle material things is an indication of how we will handle true riches. What are true riches? He doesn't say, but we know they are valuable! Perhaps they are things we can't see like biblical values, spiritual truth, and the souls of others. If we are faithful with material things, He tells us, then true spiritual wealth will follow.

Jesus also says the way we handle other people's property is a test of whether we will be given our own. When I asked the Korean lady why she returned twenty-five cents, she blushed and said simply, "It didn't belong to me."

Make no mistake: money decisions are spiritual—even in little areas! Take a moment to examine your own financial integrity. In your travel reports, do you exaggerate or "guesstimate" reimbursements for tips at the airport, quick meals, or snacks? Do you fudge your business miles on your mileage claims? Do you report actual deductions on your 1040 tax form or do you just "approximate"?

Does it matter? Of course it does, according to Luke 6:11.Unfortunately, the way we handle money in our society is not considered a spiritual issue. We believers tend to split our Christian lives into the sacred and the secular. Bible reading, prayer, church attendance, honesty, and even hard work are considered spiritual. But money is not.

Jesus disagrees. He says the way we handle "mammon" is an indication of our faithfulness to the Lord.

A friend in the Midwest worked for a business equipment company, and because he was a believer, he was given the "church accounts." Nobody else wanted to work with them because these pastors and Christian leaders didn't pay their bills on time and ignored late fees. Needless to say, the salespeople in that company were not impressed with the Christian witness they received from those clients.

Maybe you are well known for your Christian faith but you owe money all over town. I don't care how wonderful your testimony is—if you are unfaithful in the use of money, your Christian witness will not be taken seriously. And more importantly, you will not be given "true riches."

A few days ago I found a $10 bill lying in the snow outside my office. I looked up to see if someone had gone in just ahead of me, but there was no one. I confess that for a fleeting second I thought, *Wow, my lucky day!* Then I came to my senses and turned it in at the front desk.

My Korean friend's simple act has had a powerful impact on me. I keep that plastic bag with the twenty-five-cent piece inside pinned to my bulletin board. It serves as a powerful reminder that financial decisions are spiritual decisions.

CHAPTER 38

if it seems right, it can't be wrong

A FEW YEARS AGO WHEN ALMA and I lived in the Midwest, a friend from California asked me to take a business contact of his named Mark to lunch. He said Mark was a believer but was going through a breakup with his wife and needed someone to talk to.

"Sure," I told him. "Glad to help."

Mark and I met at an upscale downtown restaurant where everyone seemed young, well-dressed, and successful. He was congenial, good-looking, easy to talk to, and seemed delighted to meet me. When our food arrived, he asked if he could lead us in prayer. He bowed his head unashamedly and I followed.

I anticipated a short, to-the-point restaurant prayer, but he prayed long and large—not only for the food, but also for America, revival, and that God would bless our time together. Impressive.

This guy seems to have spiritual depth, I told myself, unfolding my napkin.

During a few minutes of small talk, Mark shared in detail his spiritual journey to Christ. Then I ventured, "Our California friend tells me you're going through marriage difficulty."

He seemed relieved to have a listening ear. "It's ugly!" he said. For the next twenty minutes he described the pain both he and his wife were going through as their trust in one another unraveled. He spoke respectfully of her but without emotion. He talked about the breakup like I talk about the dying aspens in my backyard—disappointed, but already planning their replacements.

What I said next I attribute to God's leading. It was one of those moments of God-insight. I blurted, "Are you seeing someone else?" My words seemed to lie squirming on the table. *Did I really say that?* I thought, cringing. *Should I apologize?*

But Mark wasn't offended. He looked me directly in the eyes and said, "As a matter of fact, I am seeing someone. My wife said that since we weren't going to make it anyway, she wanted me to get out more. So I'm dating an old friend. It's great!"

"Do you always take bad advice?" I queried, emboldened. "Maybe your wife was testing you to see if you really loved her."

"No, she really wanted me to date." Then he described how wonderful his new girlfriend made him feel.

I was on a roll. "Don't you think you should wait until the divorce is final before you launch into a serious dating relationship?"

"No, I really enjoy being with her, and she enjoys me, too."

Silence.

Again, I sensed a leading from God. "Are you sleeping with her?" I asked. Normally, I am not so confrontational—honest!

He again looked me in the eyes and replied unemotionally, "Yes, I am."

"Shouldn't you at least stop sleeping with her until you marry her?" I pressed.

"Oh, I have no intention of marrying," he replied. "I've been married twice already. Why do that again?"

I was incredulous. "Well, doesn't the Bible say something about that? I mean, about sex outside of marriage?"

"Does it?" He shrugged. "Where?"

I was so stunned I couldn't speak. It was time for him to return to work, so we said our good-byes. As I drove away from the restaurant, Mark's cavalier attitude got hold of me, and I began to seethe. Mini-sermons I wished I'd preached to him sprang to mind. I reminded myself, *Just because something feels right doesn't mean it is right, no matter how many years you've been "walking with Christ."*

What happened to Mark? He still attends church and sometimes sings in the choir.

Unfortunately, as Mark's story illustrates, misbehavior often seems okay to the "misbehavee," Christians included. Never mind that misbehavee is not a word—you get the point. Mark's desire for companionship and sex overpowered whatever Bible doctrine he possessed. Here's another way of saying it: *Mark's morality shaped his theology.*

As a new believer in Christ years ago, I was strongly influenced by a godly preacher who constantly reminded us with a pounding fist, "Sound doctrine equals sound living!" Today, I'm not sure that formula always works. As a middle-aged, church-attending, restaurant-praying, choir-singing Christian, Mark knew plenty of sound doctrine.

What about you and me? Does our theology guide our personal choices? Or is it the other way around? For instance, most Christians believe divorce is wrong except under rare circumstances. Yet the divorce rate in the United States for believers is as high as that of nonbelievers.

What about our attitudes toward ministry? The Bible commands us to care for the poor. Many affluent evangelicals give money to the less fortunate at Christmastime, but most don't make the effort to befriend even a single poor person the other months of the year.

Homosexuality? The Bible clearly calls it wrong, but some Christian gays interpret David's famous friendship with Jonathan as a proof text to justify their lifestyles (see 2 Samuel 1:26).

Maybe the reason we are so liberal with our theology is pain—emotional pain. When the Christian life doesn't work the way we think it is supposed to, we often reexamine our theology and rearrange it to fit our values. That's what Mark did. And that's what you and I can be tempted to do as well.

When we live in defeat, worrying about our kids or lusting after someone else's nice house, we do not want to hear Jesus' words "Do not worry" or God's commandment "Do not covet." On the contrary, we look for verses in the Bible that justify our position.

The prophet Isaiah said it well: "This people draw near with their words and honor Me with lip service, but they remove their hearts far from Me" (Isaiah 29:13).

Praying big prayers won't do it.

spiritual growth starts with your thinking

YOU MADE IT! YOU'VE WADED THROUGH thirty-eight misconceptions that can block your spiritual growth and steal your joy. Okay, now what?

Instead of trying to increase your joy thirty-eight ways by tomorrow night, ask the Holy Spirit to guide you to two or three misconceptions that strike home. Perhaps He already has. But don't make a "do-list" to improve! Rather, replace those misconceptions with truth. Otherwise, you'll end up working harder for less joy.

You are not under obligation to hang on to ineffective misconceptions. Think differently, even if the differences are minor. Well-worn cow paths crisscrossing the pasture are there because of repeated thought patterns. Frankly, it's easier to stay within those familiar ruts and grooves. But to grow spiritually, jump out of the cow paths with gusto. Remember that the apostle Paul said you will "be transformed by the renewing of your mind" (Romans 12:2). Spiritual growth starts with changing the way you think—even in small ways.

At first, your new ways of thinking may scare you. For example, if you skip reading your gotta-do-it-every-day devotional and simply meditate on one verse for fifteen minutes, you might feel guilty or think you displeased God. But go back to the misconception and correct it. In this case, the point is to sincerely worship the Lord whether you make it through your reading program or not.

You can do this. Get beyond those time-worn and misguided pathways, and start moving toward a new pasture.

Notes

Introduction: AIRPORT ROAD DOESN'T LEAD TO THE AIRPORT
1. Dallas Willard, *The Spirit of the Disciplines* (San Francisco: Harper, 1988).

Chapter 1: HAVING A BELIEF SYSTEM IS ENOUGH
1. Douglas Steele, *The Practice of the Presence of God* (Nashville: The Upper Room, 1950), 24.

Chapter 3: TO BE TRANSFORMED, FOCUS ON BEHAVIOR MODIFICATION
1. George Barna, *Growing True Disciples* (Colorado Springs, CO: WaterBrook Press, 2001), 96.
2. Barna, 75.
3. Dallas Willard, *The Spirit of the Disciplines* (San Francisco: Harper, 1988), 23.

Chapter 4: SPIRITUAL DISCIPLINES: WORK, WORK, WORK
1. J.D. Douglas, *The New International Dictionary of the Christian Church* (Grand Rapids, MI: Zondervan, 1974), 733.
2. Douglas, 905.
3. Dallas Willard, *The Spirit of the Disciplines* (San Francisco: Harper, 1988), 156.
4. Gary Thomas, *Not the End but the Road* (Colorado Springs, CO: NavPress, 2004), 18.

Chapter 5: Growing in Prayer: I've Already Tried
1. Richard Foster and Emilie Griffin, *Spiritual Classics* (San Francisco: HarperSanFrancisco, 2000), 6.

Chapter 9: Ogling Women Is a "Guy Thing"—It Can't Be Helped
1. Philip Yancey, *Rumors of Another World: What on Earth Are We Missing?* (Grand Rapids, MI: Zondervan, 2003).
2. Pornography Statistics 2003; Internet Filter Review; www.internet-filterreview.com/internet-pornography-statistics.html
3. *Business Week*, May 17, 2004. Data from ComScore Networks on U.S. Internet habits. Reported in *Discipleship Journal*, September–October 2004, 16.

Chapter 11: Only Your Spiritual Service Makes a Difference in the World
1. Frank E. Gabelein, *The Expositor's Bible Commentary*, vol. 10, "Romans–Galatians" (Grand Rapids, MI: Regency Reference Library, 1976), 207.
2. Rueben P. Job and Norman Shawchuck, *A Guide to Prayer* (Nashville: The Upper Room, 1983), 263.

Chapter 13: Sharing Your Faith Will Always Be an Awkward "Have-to"
1. George Barna, *Growing True Disciples* (Colorado Springs, CO: Waterbrook Press, 2001), 61.

Chapter 17: Everyone Worries Sometimes—What's the Big Deal?
1. William Barclay, *The Daily Bible Study Series*, vol. 1, "Matthew" (Philadelphia: Westminster Press, 1975), 261.
2. Mike Gorman, *Every Other Bed* (Nashville, Tenn.: World Publishing, 1956).
3. Ralph Waldo Emerson, *Essays: First Series. Friendship*, as quoted in Bartlett's Familiar Quotations, 16th ed. (Boston: Little, Brown, 1992), 432.

Chapter 20: Sure, you're Busy — It's Unavoidable
1. Richard Swenson, *The Overload Syndrome* (Colorado Springs, CO: Navpress, 1998), 126.
2. Swenson, 123.
3. Mimi Doe, *Busy But Balanced: Practical and Inspirational Ways to Create a Calmer, Closer Family* (New York: St. Martin's Press, 2001).

Chapter 21: You Need to Be Available 24/7
1. Thomas S. Kepler, *Pathways to Spiritual Power* (Cleveland, OH: The World Publishing Company, 1952), 103.

Chapter 22: You Can't Help But Be a Little Judgmental
1. W.E. Vine, *Expository Dictionary of New Testament Words* (Old Tappan, NJ: Fleming H. Revell Company, 1966), 280.

Chapter 24: Leadership Is Primarily Talking
1. Lewis C. Henry, *Best Quotations for all Occasions* (Greenwich, CT: Fawcett Publications Inc, 1959), 135.

Chapter 29: You Are What You Look Like
1. Bill Radford, "Trading Faces," *Colorado Springs Gazette*, Life section, December 30, 2002, 3.

Chapter 32: Tithing Is the Standard
1. George Barna, *Growing True Disciples* (Colorado Springs, CO: WaterBrook Press, 2001), 74.
2. C. S. Lewis, *Virtue and Vice: A Dictionary of the Good Life* (New York: Harper Collins, 2005), 4.

Chapter 33: Skipping Church Is No Big Deal
1. George Barna, *Growing True Disciples* (Colorado Springs, CO: WaterBrook Press, 2001), 59.

About the Author

SCOTT MORTON SERVES WITH THE NAVIGATORS as Vice President of Development for U.S. ministries. He graduated from Iowa State University in technical journalism and worked in newspaper advertising before joining the Navigators staff in 1970. Previous assignments include Columbia, Missouri; Iowa City, Iowa; Madison, Wisconsin; Minneapolis, Minnesota; and summer ministries in Asia and Europe. He has served in Development since 1985.

Scott and his wife, Alma, met the Lord through The Navigators' ministry at Iowa State. They have been married since 1964 and have two married daughters, one married son, and four grandchildren.

The Mortons enjoy baseball (Scott was drafted by the Baltimore Orioles and Minnesota Twins), bird-watching, antiquing, and helping people grow in their spiritual journeys through small-group Bible studies and one-on-one mentoring. Scott also enjoys writing, having published *Funding Your Ministry (Whether You're Gifted or Not)*, a book to help missionaries raise financial support, and *Down to Earth Discipling,* a realistic approach to sharing one's faith.

EXPERIENCE THE AUTHENTIC JOY
OF CHRIST.

The Lost Virtue of Happiness

J. P. Moreland
and Klaus Issler   1-57683-648-7

Our hunger for immediate gratification leaves us
with an "empty self." Through profound advice
and personal stories, the authors show you how the
ancient spiritual disciplines can turn your focus back
to God and experience true joy.

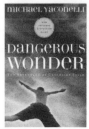

Restless Faith

Winn Collier   1-57683-711-4

When you cannot understand the ways of God,
embrace the mystery and let your restless faith lead
you on a great adventure to the edges of belief, hope,
and transformation.

Dangerous Wonder

Mike Yaconelli   1-57683-481-6

If you're looking for the joy and freedom of faith, this
book will open your eyes and your life to the exciting
adventure of a relationship with God.

Visit your local Christian bookstore,
call NavPress at 1-800-366-7788, or log on to www.navpress.com.
To locate a Christian bookstore near you, call 1-800-991-7747.

NAVPRESS

BRINGING TRUTH TO LIFE

www.navpress.com